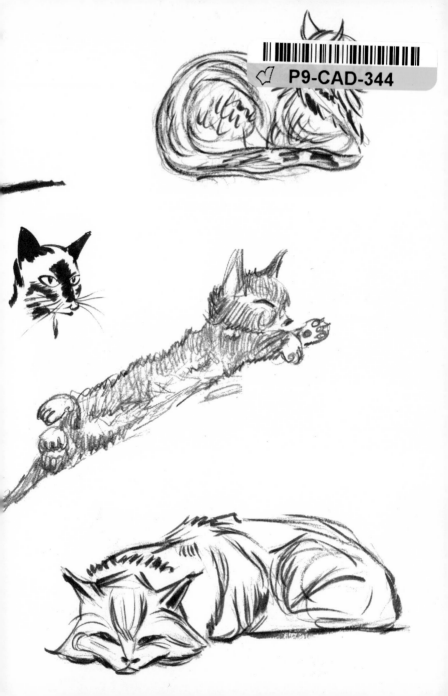

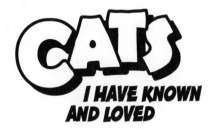

CATS
I HAVE KNOWN AND LOVED

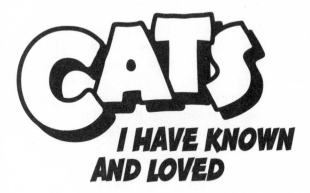

CATS
I HAVE KNOWN AND LOVED

PIERRE BERTON

with illustrations by the author

DOUBLEDAY CANADA

Doubleday Canada and colophon are trademarks.

National Library of Canada Cataloguing in Publication Data

Berton, Pierre, 1920–

Cats I have known and loved / Pierre Berton.

ISBN 0-385-65938-5

1. Cats—Anecdotes. 2. Berton, Pierre, 1920–
3. Cat owners—Canada—Biography. I. Title.

SF445.5.B47 2002   636.8'088'7   C2002-902065-4

Jacket photography: Joseph Amaral
Printed and bound in Canada

Published in Canada by
Doubleday Canada, a division of
Random House of Canada Limited

Visit Random House of Canada Limited's website:
www.randomhouse.ca

FRI 10 9 8 7 6 5 4 3 2

THIS BOOK IS DEDICATED TO:

Potty, Happy, Pieface, Brownie, Sebastienne, Snowball,
Punkoo, Marmalade, Sari, Simon, Paprika, Puss,
Meow Tse-Tung, Winston, Julian, Whisper, Calpurnia, Og,
Sushi, Eros, Agapé, Nefer, Loki, Pandora, Candy, Matthew,
Cougar, Dave, Candy #2, Alice, Rhoda, Lois, Tchin-Tchin,
Fluffy, Midas, Pookie, Dave, Pyramus, Thisbe, Cressida,
Ignatius, Party, Cecil, Hamilton Beach, Wally Simpson, Ruby,
Clyde, Tail Light, Spooky, Pousse-Pousse, and Suki.

CONTENTS

PROLOGUE

The Mystery of the Vanishing Cat

OVERLEAF: *Pousse-Pousse, at peace with himself after his long adventure*

CATS ARE THE ULTIMATE SURVIVORS. THEY TRULY HAVE NINE lives, and they are careful to use them up sparingly. Once they have ceased to be kittens they are on their own and they know it. Their mother becomes a stranger, totally disinterested in their welfare. Their credo is simple: *Look after number one!*

We know all those dog stories—the faithful canine standing guard over his master's body, refusing to eat, resisting all efforts to pull him away. Such fealty is not for cats. The master of the house may topple to the kitchen floor clutching at his heart, but the family cat will walk over his prostrate form to gobble a saucer of milk. And all the while he is watching over his shoulder in case some predator is lurking round the corner. That's why cats survive.

My favourite cat survivor story comes from my neighbours, the Gordons, next door. *Next door?* Their home, on the rim of the Humber Valley is actually several hundred yards from our own. They look out, as we do, on a small forest of pointed Christmas trees—white cedars that clothe the slopes leading down to the river. Here, the Humber Valley stretches off to the north, a misty, evergreen realm, the home of wild coyotes, foxes, raccoons, and small herds of deer who follow the river and use the valley as protection. Sometimes they venture up the slopes to gnaw at the bark of newly planted birch and poplar trees on my front lawn. I forgive them, for the sight of a delicate little doe and her two speckled fawns is worth the grief.

It was in this environment that the next-door cat performed his vanishing act. He was, in many ways, a crazy, mixed-up cat. He had two names, which suggests the two distinct sides of his personality, a not-unknown quality in cats. Lying on the living room couch, slobbering away and purring loudly, he was a feline Dr. Jekyll. Creeping through the undergrowth below the house and pouncing savagely on small mice, voles, and even chipmunks, he was Mr. Hyde—the terror of the neighbourhood.

He was already a survivor when our neighbour's daughter, Julie, found him abandoned in a ditch, a lost kitten mewing hungrily for room service. Julie, who was stabling her horse in a nearby barn, turned the kitten over to an accommodating mother cat, who licked him down furiously and looked after him as well as she did her own tribe. There, the cat bonded with Julie's horse, Sydney, snuggling up to him for warmth and putting his nose against Sydney's, almost as if he was kissing him. Later on, the memory of that would help the cat to survive.

The kitten eventually grew to adulthood and moved into Julie's parents' home. She called him Killer, a name that reflects his hobby of ripping the hides off small furry animals. But when the family moved to their new house near us on the rim of the Humber Valley, her mother balked at the prospect of having to shout "Here Killer, Killer!" across the fields. She discarded the outdoor name and opted for an indoor name: "Pousse-Pousse." That too presented a problem. In our area, if you shout "Here Pousse-Pousse" out the door, half a dozen assorted felines turn up, expecting a handout. Everybody I know calls their cat "Puss" more often than not. The cats don't know the difference because they think "Puss" and "Pousse-Pousse" are synonyms for lunch.

Inside the house, the killer cat turned into a bit of a wimp. When he wasn't creeping through the forest, he was stretched out on the living room sofa, yawning in his sleep. No hint of a killer instinct there. When he had nothing else to do, he padded down the hall and into the bathroom, sat in the empty bathtub, or even curled up and went to sleep. Cats, as we all know, seek out confined spaces. It gives them a false sense of security. Later, in this memoir, you will encounter Ruby, my tabby, who likes to curl up in a wooden salad bowl that seems to have been especially designed for her; and also Spooky, who snoozes in my in-basket, a move that plays havoc with my personal papers. Any cardboard box, filing cabinet, cupboard, drawer, pail or tub is fair game for house cats.

Surrounded, on at least three sides, safe from fancied predators, they feel protected. We have had several cats who, on arriving at our place, check out the bathroom, discover the bidet, and immediately climb into it. It's not just that they seek protection; they are also insatiably curious.

Pousse-Pousse, a.k.a. Killer, didn't really have to hunt for food. He would leave the bathtub, stroll into the kitchen, and mew for a handout. A stubborn cat, who wouldn't take no for an answer, he had learned to get someone's attention by nosing them, as he had once nosed Julie's horse, Sydney, back in the barn.

He was a special cat because, unlike your average tabby, he had six toes, complete with claws. His feet were like snowshoes, and that came in handy in the winter, when he would slide across the ice on the driveway or pond, or pad over the crusted snow. He liked to show off by using his extra toes to pick up a ball, a trick at which he became especially adept.

The extra toes, I think, convinced him that he was not really like other cats. They gave him an edge in the mouse-catching business, and Pousse-Pousse, in his killer role, was one terrific mouser. He maintained an enviable collection of mouse tails, which turned up in chinks and crannies and also baskets and sofas about the house. Of that collection, the six-toed cat was justifiably proud. I suspect that he considered himself indestructible, a dangerous assumption as it turned out.

Vain? You bet he was vain. One day a partridge struck the Gordons' picture window and fell to the ground. Pousse-Pousse pounced on it, carried it proudly into the living room, laid it at Julie Gordon's feet, and pretended he'd killed it. Julie insisted that he believed he *had* killed it. Her mother gave it to us, and Janet and I had it for dinner.

There are three types of house cats: the inside cat, the outside cat, and the in-and-out cat. Pousse-Pousse belonged to the last and most crowded category. He would stand at the front door and meow to be let out. A little later, having been released, he would stand outside the same door and meow to be let back in. There is no ignoring in-and-out cats; they are totally in charge, and you must indulge them.

When he was outside, Pousse-Pousse would creep through the tall grass and explore his way through the forest below the house, past the wild apple orchard and the new crop of fiddle-head ferns beneath the cedars until he roamed as far as the banks of the river itself. The river was high that spring, a rushing torrent fed by the melting snow pouring in streams down the slopes. In my garden the Nanking cherries were in bloom—a soft pink cloud against the cloudless sky. The first daffodils were popping open, and in the woods the perfect white flowers of the big-leafed bloodroot could be spotted. Across the river, a vast meadow of white trilliums, interspersed with their darker red varieties, enlivened the pathway.

So now we come to that fateful April day. Exhausted from his prowling and taking his ease on the Gordons' patio, Pousse-Pousse was a cat without a care in the world—a cat so sure of himself that he would lie stretched out, eyes shut, soaking up the spring sunshine, oblivious to the world around him.

The view from this spot is exquisite. In the morning, soft mists rise from the hidden river, clothing the cedars in a filmy mantle. In the evening, the dying sun briefly anoints their upper branches with a film of gold. Not that Pousse-Pousse gave a hoot. He slept with confidence, secure in the belief that he was safe.

The sun was high in the cloudless sky when something happened—an almost mystic moment that Julie would never forget. Suddenly Pousse-Pousse wasn't there! She had seen him from the window curled up on his side. A minute later, she looked again and he had vanished—poof!—as if a stage magician had waved his wand to make him disappear. One moment he was snoozing away; the next he was gone, without a trace, leaving no clue, no hint, not so much as a whisper as to his sudden absence.

Where was he? What had happened to him? Had he got up, stretched himself, and wandered off down the driveway only to be hit by a passing car? The time frame didn't allow for that. Julie asked around, but nobody had seen any signs of such a mishap. Had he crept once too often into the forest, to be eaten by a prowling coyote? If so, where was the *corpus delecti?* She combed the valley looking for clues. There were none.

Week after week the search went on. Every driveway, every country lane, every ditch was searched in the grisly possibility that a six-toed corpse might be mouldering out of sight. Nothing. Had something happened to cause him to run away from home? Surely not. He was a stay-at-home cat who liked his life as it was, snoozing on the sofa and in the bathtub and padding off for kitchen goodies when the mood struck him. Julie was convinced that he was out there somewhere, very much alive, but constrained by circumstances, unable to reach her. The maddening thing was the absence of any clue as to his fate; it was a muddy April, but there was no sign of a six-toed paw print to suggest where Pousse-Pousse had gone.

The months dragged on, but the cat did not come back. In the valley, the apples and hawthorns blossomed.

Jack-in-the-pulpits raised their striped heads above the grasses. On the riverbank, May apples bloomed beneath the poplars, their exquisite flowers hidden under the broad leaves. Small sandbars appeared along the bank where the bottle gentians grew. Wild blackberries glistened in the sunlight; small birds ate them greedily. But still there was no sign of Pousse-Pousse.

Autumn came, and the wild grapes began to ripen on the tangle of vines in the forest. The leaves of the sumac turned bright red. Cold breezes blew down from the Northwest, loosening the maple and alder leaves that drifted across the spot where Pousse-Pousse had once lain, stretched out in the sun. But still there was not the slightest hint as to what had happened. Was he out there somewhere? Julie was starting to lose hope.

It began to snow. Once again, the pointed cedars in the valley looked like Christmas trees bedecked with cotton batting. Little shivering mice found their way into the Gordons' kitchen and hid in the cupboards. They became bold because there was no Pousse-Pousse on hand to chase them off or collect their tails. On the margins of the river, a thin sheet of ice began to form. More snow fell. The ice thickened and crept out from the shore until the river was as hard as concrete. By now, even Julie was convinced her cat was dead.

And then, one chill November morning, Julie heard a small squeak outside her bedroom door, which opened directly onto the deck. She opened it, and there was the sorriest-looking cat she had ever encountered. He was as thin as a pencil—all skin and bone. One forepaw had been broken and had healed badly. His ragged fur was matted, and his stomach was so distended it looked as if he'd swallowed a balloon.

Was it—*could* it be—Pousse-Pousse? She held her breath. The cat made a feeble jump onto a side table and gave out a familiar "e-eek!" It must be her cat! That was certainly his voice. She picked him up—all bones and light as thistledown now—cuddled him and examined his misshapen paw. *Six toes!* After seven months, her beloved cat had come home at last.

But where had he been all that time? What had happened to him? Why was he in this dreadful condition? It was an enigma that required all the ingenuity of a private eye to unravel. At last, with the help of the local veterinarian, Julie began to figure it out.

The vet found two deep scars on the cat's head and another under his chin. Obviously something had ripped into him. Were these claw marks? If so, they had a clue at last. The former Killer had left no tell-tale tracks because he had been lifted off his resting place and carried away by another killer—a winged predator with razor-sharp claws. A hawk? That was unlikely. Even the common red-tail, which circled restlessly above the valley on clear days, scarcely had the wing power to fly off with anything larger than a squirrel. Only one bird of prey could have brought it off. Pousse-Pousse's captor had been a big owl, probably a great horned.

It must have been an awesome spectacle: the owl flapping, even staggering above the trees with his oversized prey dangling and struggling in his grip. In the end, the bird would have been forced to sink lower and lower into the valley until the cat broke free and tumbled earthward. That certainly explained the broken paw, which had healed so badly that it had to be broken again and then straightened out.

But why hadn't Pousse-Pousee come limping home? It dawned on Julie that he couldn't *get* home, because the big bird had managed to carry him as far as the Humber River, whose turbulent waters constituted an implacable barrier, and must have dropped him on the far side.

That made sense, for the cat had returned almost as soon as the river froze. What a trip that must have been—to claw his way down river and up the valley slope for half a mile or more! It was obvious that he had been dropped well upstream, far from the nearest house, far beyond the fields of trilliums and the swamps ablaze with yellow marsh marigolds. As I know

Pousse-Pousse, after his reunion with old friends

from my long hikes along its banks, the Humber was devoid of human habitat as a result of the ravages of Hurricane Hazel. This was a remote and tangled realm, a home for coyotes, whose litters we could hear yelping each spring, for deer, who gnawed away at the young saplings each winter, and for beaver, who stubbornly repaired their broken dams each year.

There, Pousse-Pousse must have made his home, and there he would have scrabbled for provender, pouncing on small mice, baby chipmunks, moles, voles, and all manner of tasty four-legged morsels—a killer, true to his name. All that became obvious after the vet took a look at his distended stomach, opened him up, and removed a gigantic fur ball, in which was mingled an agglomeration of small bones, hide, tiny claws, teeth, and hair. For seven months that had been his meagre diet.

Had he found any shelter from the rain, from the cloud-bursts that swept down the valley in the summer, and from the snow flurries of the early fall? Julie Gordon discovered one more clue a short time after he returned. A covey of deer wandered up through the cedars and came to rest on the lawn, just below the big window where Pousse-Pousse liked to sun himself. Julie heard them and opened the door to the deck, and there they were. As she stepped back, Pousse-Pousse rushed out to greet them, trotted over to the nearest deer and planted a kiss on his nose, just as he had once smooched Sydney, the friendly horse. The deer seemed delighted to see him, and there was no doubt about his long absence. He had lived with the herd, probably sleeping with them in the cold nights, secure in the warmth of a fellow animal.

That all happened some years ago. Pousse-Pousse still lives in the house next door, but by now, he is an older and wiser cat. He no longer thinks of himself as Killer. He prefers a new role: World's Most Lovable Cat. He crawls all over visitors, rolling on the rug, stretching out his neck to be tickled, demanding affection. He purrs a lot, and he still likes to snooze in the bathtub. What he seems to be saying, as he lets himself be picked up and cuddled, is "I'm so glad to be home." When the sun is shining, he wanders outside and stretches in the long grass below the deck. But he has learned that he is not invincible and so he keeps one half-closed eye on any small creatures that might scurry by and the other fixed on the sky above—the home of hovering predators waiting to pounce on unsuspecting prey.

As for Julie, she has since grown to adulthood, married, and taken on a lifetime career. Not surprisingly, she has become a veterinarian.

Pousse-Pousse snuggling a baby rabbit some years after his adventure. No Killer, he.

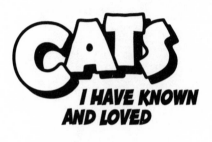

ONE

Cats of My Childhood

MY FIRST CAT WAS A TINY BLACK AND WHITE KITTEN THAT MY parents brought to our small bungalow in Dawson City, Yukon Territory. I cannot now remember whether he was a white cat with black spots, or a black cat with white spots, but I do remember his name: Spotty. I was four at the time, and my sister was fifteen months younger; neither of us could manage the "S" sound, so we called him "Potty," an apt name, as it turned out, but an unfortunate one since, being badly house-trained, he went potty on my mother's prized Persian rug once too often. That was the end of him. He simply disappeared, and we asked no questions, though I remember connecting my father in some way with his absence.

For the next decade I was without a real cat. Instead I lived with fantasy felines, quirky anthropomorphic creatures, endlessly fascinating, always bewitching, and generally astonishing—the pen-and-ink cats who gambolled through the comic pages, or the "funnies" as we called them.

These cats of my childhood, who seemed more real to me than the unfortunate Potty, luxuriated in what we now realize was the golden age of the comics, when newspapers competed to grab as many strips as possible for their weekend supplements. My own ambition, in those early years, was to be a comic strip artist. I tried to copy the characters, including the cats, who romped through the comic pages so that by the time I reached high school I was on the way to becoming a passable cartoonist. That is another story; suffice to say, I learned to draw cats, some of whom appear in these pages.

In my youth the comics really *were* comic. To a growing boy, reared in a small, isolated community, where even radio was unknown, the funny papers provided a window, albeit distorted, on that magic world we called "The Outside"—a world of skyscrapers and choo-choo trains, three-ring circuses and Ferris wheels, big department stores, sun-drenched beaches complete with sand castles, and sleek, eight-cylinder automobiles operated by sleeker eight-cylinder movie stars. In short, the comic pages provided us with everything we didn't have in the frozen North, from crowded racetracks (*Barney Google*) to soda fountains (*Harold Teen*) to electric trolley cars (*Toonerville Folks*).

The comic pages of those days did not feature many dogs. The few mutts who appeared in such juvenile strips as *Jus' Kids* and *Reg'lar Fellers* seemed to me to be devoid of any personality. They remained in the background, part of the scenery, members of the gang, but without any endearing qualities. The comic strip cats were different. Each was unique, each was quirky, each was a character. So indeed was my eighty-year-old grandfather, a journalist of renown and also a humourist, who had worked on all of the Toronto papers and had contributed regularly to the satirical weekly *Grip*. He made a regular practice of shipping me a huge bundle of the Sunday comics from his home in Oakville. Not having a cat of my own, I bonded with the ones that romped through the funnies, and I think their presence had a good deal to do with the flesh-and-blood cats that later took over my life.

I'm not sure why the comic strip dogs were not appealing. Maybe it was just me. Or maybe the dog lovers who read the comics didn't want liberties taken with their pets—didn't want the stereotype of the faithful dog caricatured. Or was it because all dogs tend to be the same—devoted, loyal and compliant to a fault. Cats, on the other hand, are capricious and unpredictable—or at least can be made to appear so without offending the great army of cat fanciers who tend to revel in their pets' eccentricities.

At first my parents refused to allow me to read these comics. They belonged to the "evil influence" school of parenthood that began in the Victorian Age when young girls were protected from reading romantic novels and that would still be going strong a century later when modern television programs would also be considered an evil influence on the nation's youth

But a tight roll of comic pages kept arriving from my grandfather, and, at last, my parents relented. As a result, some of my happiest childhood memories are of those bright summer mornings when I slept out on our front porch and occupied my early waking hours devouring page after coloured page, following the adventures of Skeezix, Moon Mullins, Andy Gump, and, best of all, a black cat named Felix who wandered alone through preposterous landscapes peopled with fantasy figures.

FELIX

For all of my childhood years, Felix was my surrogate cat, and, in my view, the most compelling of the five feline protagonists who could be found scampering about in the comic pages my grandfather sent. Felix began life as an animated cat in a series of inspired one-reel cartoons. He made his Hollywood debut in 1917, but movies took so long to reach Dawson in those days that I like to feel I was in on the beginning.

I still remember my delight when the smart black cat, teetering on a line of washing suspended between two buildings, tried vainly to reach out for a bottle of milk sitting on a window ledge. His tail was not long enough to dip into the milk, and the usual question mark appeared above Felix's head. The ingenious cat reached for the symbol, attached it to his tail and managed to extend it. To my delight, he dipped his newly lengthened tail into the bottle, retrieved it, sucked out the milk and repeated the process until the bottle was empty. Not long after that, Felix, having established himself as a movie star, moved to the comic pages. For a small boy growing up in an isolated backwater, he was the perfect companion, especially when he became enmeshed in a long series of fantasy adventures. He visited Mother Gooseland, found himself thrust into the mechanized civilization of the future, and travelled to the planets of the solar system and to the savage jungles of Africa. When he spoke, a square balloon above his head carried his words to his fans, and Felix was not above reaching up for that balloon to use it as a weapon to thwart miscreants.

This little black cat with the white face and huge googly eyes, who walked upright on two feet, was separated by a country mile from the cheerful Disneyesque creatures who were beginning to invade the movie screens. It is said that Felix's character was inspired by Kipling's tale, *The Cat Who Walks By Himself.* Certainly he walked alone throughout his many adventures, and it was this loneliness that his followers found so hauntingly appealing. Maurice Horn, an expert on early comic strips, has pointed out that Felix brought to the comic pages the environment of the animated cartoon—"the poetry of its strange landscapes, its flight into the world of the dream, the melancholy of deserted forests and roads in which he wanders under the low hanging full moon." A kindred spirit for a boy wandering down the ghostly streets of a dying mining town, or clambering up through the gloomy forests of its surrounding hills.

For Felix was the quintessential wanderer, as so many of his flesh and blood kin are as well. "Felix kept on walking, kept on walking still"—so went the lyrics of a hit tune of the day that had everybody humming. In France his impact was even greater than in North America. "Felix is not a cat," Marcel Brion, a French academician, has written. "He is *the* cat, or better yet to say, he is a supercat, because he does not fit into any of the categories of the animal kingdom."

There was a depth to Felix that I dimly sensed, and that, in later years, I have sometimes noticed in some members of the varied feline menagerie who have allowed me to admire them. Horn calls him "one of the great creations of modern art." The clichés of various animal strips never invaded the page devoted to Felix. In the midst of the dreamlike fantasies that enchanted us in the twenties, there was a solid underpinning of reality. Felix's world was not a safe and friendly one.

As Horn puts it, "his loneliness, his sense of alienation, and his obstinate fight against fate, the elements, thunder, cold, and an uncaring and callous humankind, mark him as an early hero of the absurd in animal guise." Even in fairyland, Felix encountered cold, indifference, and absurdity as stray cats often do. That is what drew me to him in later years, and that is why, when in the midst of a rainstorm my wife and I saw a strange feline face pressed against our window, howling for help, we let her in and allowed her to have her kittens in our bedroom closet.

 **KRAZY KAT**

After my family left the North and moved to Victoria, B.C., in the early thirties, I became aware of another comic strip about a cat who walked on two legs and, like Felix, operated in a weird world of fantasy. But Krazy Kat bore no more resemblance to Felix than does a caribou to an ostrich.

This cat defied all logic—but then, what cat doesn't? The setting was bizarre; a cat existing in the great American desert, a whimsical realm of pipe dreams, whose stark background of angular shapes changed from panel to panel so that a mesa would be transformed into a steamboat for no apparent reason, or a palm tree might suddenly appear to shade the Kat without explanation.

The influence of the famous and controversial Armoury Show of 1913, which introduced French Impressionism and German expressionism to the American public, was percolating down to the comic strip. I had never heard of it, but I was certainly dazzled by the revolutionary approach of the Kat's creator, George Herriman, and by his equally revolutionary Kat.

The story-line defied common sense, turning conventional situations upside down. Here was a dog—"Offisa Pup"—deeply in love with a Kat. Here was a Kat, madly in love with a mouse. Here was a mouse—Ignatz—whose only satisfaction was to fling a brick at the Kat, knocking her senseless and creating a halo not of comic strip stars, but of little throbbing hearts. While this is transpiring, the ever-watchful Pup tries to protect his beloved who doesn't wish to be protected because she sees the brick itself as a symbol of affection. That, in brief, is the basis for the eternal triangle, which lasted for thirty years.

This topsy-turvy plot line was an allegory. "Ignatz Mouse and Offisa Pup are society's age-old antagonists, the rebel and the policeman," George Sorel, himself a cartoonist, has pointed out. "Neither can understand Krazy because Krazy is a creature of infinite love, while they can only understand *power*. For them, might makes right. For Krazy, *love conquers all*."

As a boy in high school, I did not understand these subtleties. But the idea of a mouse turning on a cat, and the cat

accepting it as an act of love, intrigued me. Like the cats I have known and loved, from Pousse-Pousse, the owl's prey, to my own Wally Simpson, a tabby who endured for 24 years, Krazy Kat was above all a survivor. In spite of her all but incomprehensible speech pattern, an unlikely combination of southern hillbilly and Bronx gangster, in spite of the daily hail of bricks, the cloying attention of the law-and-order Pup, the cynical scorn of the eternally frustrated mouse, the Kat prevailed.

The strip became the most highly praised of all. In 1929, she was the subject of a full-length ballet. Woodrow Wilson would never let a day pass without absorbing the latest episode in the Kat's saga. Yet the strip never made a profit and would have been dropped if the syndicate owner, William Randolph Hearst, a devoted fan, had not insisted it be published without interference.

Here we come to the final absurdity in this galaxy of paradoxes. The very people who might have taken the Kat to their bosoms were members of that sophisticated tribe who had no use for Hearst's yellow journalism. At its peak, no more than three dozen papers carried the strip, leaving the Kat standing alone in a Hearstian desert, in its creator's words, "a vagabond and an explorer of those regions of illusion that only the winds cross by day and the moon beams reveal by night." To me that applies not only to Krazy and Felix, but to all the cats I have known—those ever-mysterious felines, who are prepared to love unconditionally, but on their own terms, who go their own way, travel their own road, keep their own counsel, and resolutely refuse to mingle with the pack.

PIERRE BERTON

ESMERELDA, SPOOKY, AND EM

Three other cats caught my eye during the golden age of the comic strip. One appeared as a minor character in the first continually published comic strip in history. This was the strip that chronicled the idiosyncrasies of A. Mutt, Bud Fisher's creation, who made his appearance in 1907 and soon acquired a partner, the bewhiskered Jeff. *Mutt and Jeff* became one of the best-known comic strips in history. Mutt acquired a son, Cicero, who quickly acquired a cat. The cat, Esmerelda, became such a hit that in 1933, during my first year in high school, Cicero's Cat acquired a strip of her own on the Mutt and Jeff Sunday page.

This was a cat who looked more like a real cat than Felix or Krazy with one difference: Her creator, Al Smith (Fisher's assistant), gave her a hat and coat to wear. But, as Bill Blackbeard, the leading historian of the comics, has remarked, Esmerelda's humanized escapades "were rarely as effective as the purely cat-like sequences."

The one comic strip cat who looked more like a real cat than its contemporaries was Spooky, the firehouse cat in Bill Holman's insanely surrealistic Sunday strip *Smokey Stover.* Spooky appeared in what Maurice Horn has called "probably the most outrageous comic strip ever devised." The loony cat, who was quickly given a strip of her own, was a shaggy and shabby black feline with white paws who walked on all fours and whose trademark was a red bandage tied around her tail.

She too was a wanderer, a roving vagabond whose quirky character fitted neatly into Holman's pun-filled world, where fire engines came equipped with tank tracks "to tread softly" and musical chimes, which replaced sirens because they were more melodic. Spooky, too, was slightly demented, but compared to the rest of the nonsensical characters who were woven into Holman's panels, she was the soul of sanity. She, too, reflected the period—a slightly battered pussy, surviving the madness around her, against all odds.

One other cartoon cat caught and held my interest in those dark, yet carefree, days. That was the strange, goggle-eyed feline who turned up regularly in Cliff Sterrett's semi-surrealistic *Polly and Her Pals.* Polly, who began life in 1912—a New Woman like Tillie the Toiler and Winnie Winkle, the Breadwinner—was a slender, long-legged brunette. But she soon found herself moved into the background of a strip that was dominated by her stubby and often frazzled parents, "Maw" and "Paw," and their ubiquitous and ever-present cat. In the 40 years that followed, the cat became a major character in the script, generally known simply as "Kitty," but also, on occasion, as "Dot" or "Em."

What fascinated me was the way the cat clung to Paw and copied his every movement. She fitted neatly into Sterrett's increasingly avant-garde style. Indeed, she acted as a kind of Greek chorus to Polly's often embattled father. If Paw clapped a hand to his forehead in despair, the cat, who never spoke, did so, too. If Paw reared back in astonishment, the soles of his feet showing in the style of the day and the word "Plop!" appearing

over his head, the cat followed suit, clasping her forehead and reeling backwards, too. If Paw hid behind a sofa in the living room, the cat hid with him, clutching the furniture as her master did. She was Paw's cat, ever by his side, following at his heels from parlour to garden, even raising her hands in the air as her master did when a masked gunman appeared, crying "This is a stickup!" I envied Paw his faithful companion: Oh! to have a cat like that—one that was completely yours, a cat to call your own. A cat who understood as you grappled with the mysteries of puberty and reached out for companionship. I yearned for such a cat, and, as it turned out, at the age of sixteen, I finally acquired one.

TWO

My First Cats

HAPPY, THE GRAVEDIGGER

I was walking west on Douglas Street in Victoria when I saw the cat and I knew at once that I had to have her. Those were the darkest years of the Depression and, at the age of sixteen, I was alone, or felt I was. My father had been forced to go back North to earn enough to support the family. Movies were ten cents, but I didn't have ten cents, only streetcar fare. And there, in the window of a pet shop, I spotted a tabby cat in a cage, looking straight at me and mewing softly. The sign on the cage read "Free to Good Home."

The cat was being harassed by chattering monkeys in neighbouring cages, who made faces at her while uttering high-pitched shrieks. She looked at me imploringly, a handsome tabby, perfectly marked, with a dark ring around her collar, and the standard V-shape on her brow. She raised her paws up against the netting and opened her mouth again, this time in a silent mew. It was a cry for help: *Please! Take me. Get me away from the torments of these weird, shrieking creatures. I promise you'll never regret it.*

I hesitated for no more than a moment as the cat tried to reach out to me. Then I walked into the store crammed with canaries, budgies, guinea pigs, puppy dogs, and other assorted would-be pets, including tanks full of goldfish. The cat followed me with her eyes and twisted about to face me. As we stared at each other I made my decision. Was she really free to a good home? I asked, because I have a good home for her. Take her, the man behind the counter said. Take her away; she doesn't belong here.

He opened the cage and out she strolled, maintaining her dignity as I reached out and picked her up. She didn't struggle. She kept her claws sheathed as I stroked her, and as I walked out the door, she nuzzled me. I tickled her under the chin, and she closed her eyes in ecstasy. I was in ecstasy too—she was mine—mine in every way. I was taking her to a good home, as the placard said, and she sensed it.

What was the cat doing in a cage at the pet store? And why, in those Depression days, when every nickel counted, was she being given away? I could only surmise that she had been purchased as a kitten from the store by owners who, for one reason or another, found they could not keep her and so returned her like an Eaton's parcel. Since she was already paid for, the store was duty bound to release her to any likely looking cat lover who happened by. That, at least, was my theory as I walked back down Douglas Street with the cat in my arms and caught the Oak Bay streetcar.

One problem concerned me. I had taken it upon myself to acquire a new member of the family without so much as a by-your-leave. How would the other members of the family react? My sister had wanted a dog, and my mother was pondering that possibility. Would she let me keep the cat, or would she insist I take it back to the store? Now, as the streetcar rattled along Oak Bay Avenue, I made a decision: Nothing would part me from my new friend, neither sibling rivalry, nor parental opposition. If necessary, I would put up a fight to keep her.

The cat in my arms didn't budge. We got off at the terminus and walked across the park to McNeill Avenue, the unpaved street where I lived. My mother and sister were out shopping. I walked up the back stairs and into the kitchen, put the cat down, poured her a saucer of Jersey milk, and stroked her cheek. She lapped at the milk and began to purr—a happy cat if there ever was one. I named her in the moment: *Happy.*

When my mother and sister returned and entered the kitchen, there she was, taking her ease as if she had been there forever. "This is Happy," I told them. If my mother had any qualms about a strange animal invading her space, she quickly put them aside. Many years later, with both her children married and long gone from the nest, Happy, the cat I had rescued, helped to rescue her from her loneliness.

In the days that followed in Victoria, Happy and I bonded, or at least I did. My father had built a long garden trellis on our property before he went back North and on that shaky plywood contrivance, built for climbing vines, the cat perched, looked down at me, and dared me to poke at her. Then she, in turn, would bat at me with one soft paw and a mock battle would begin.

We would chase each other across the lawn and the back vegetable garden. She would wait for me behind a shrub, pounce out, then roll over and curl up as cats do when they want to be poked and patted. Then she would scamper off and clamber up the trellis or the gate at the front door or one of the ornamental trees and dare me to poke at her again. She liked attention and didn't mind being roughed up, like Krazy Kat, who yearned for Ignatz's brick. For her too it was a sign of affection and, for me, love.

She slept with me most nights, cuddling up under the covers, raising her head so I could scratch her under the chin, and following me downstairs to the kitchen at breakfast. There was no such thing as kitty litter—certainly not in our house—but Happy had her own methods. When she was stuck in the house

at night, she would saunter into the bathroom, jump into the tub, and squat over the drain to answer the call of nature. We could not afford cat food in those days; indeed, I didn't know anybody who could. Happy ate scraps saved from the table, or sometimes "bones for the dog," which we obtained from our local butcher—a standard practice in the Hungry Thirties. My mother made soup from the bones but saved a bit of the meat for Happy. The butcher was never fooled. He knew we had no dog; but he didn't realize we did have a hungry cat.

Though she was almost full grown when I found her, she still had a lot of kitten in her. But the time soon came when the big Toms with the torn ears howled on the back fence. She would leave my bed, slip out of the house, and prowl the back alleys, dallying with her many suitors.

Was I a jealous lover? Quite the opposite. I feared for her safety, out there in the gloom. I lay in my bed haunted by unknown terrors. What if she were run over by a passing car? What if some wild beast attacked her? What if she took ill and died? I could not bear the prospect and tried to dismiss it from my mind, but it recurred and I felt the agony of her loss. If anything happened to my cat, I told myself, I would not be able to bear it. I loved her with a passion, and I could feel the knife in my heart when I contemplated a future without her.

But she survived to produce innumerable kittens of every colour and design. Like all tabbies of my acquaintance, she was a wonderful mother. For the first few days, she never left

OPPOSITE: *Happy on the trellis, daring me to play*

the box where she nurtured her new offspring. Then she would move them to a new location, as cats do—not once, but three times. If they were born in my mother's closet on the top floor, after three or four days, she would carry them by the scruff of the neck in her mouth, downstairs, one at a time. After she had removed all the kittens, she would trot back upstairs, mewing plaintively for another. But there was no other. I had been conditioned by the comic strips to believe cats were half human, like Cicero, with his jacket, or Felix, who walked upright. Now, it dawned on me that cats cannot count.

Happy was always convinced that another kitten existed somewhere—one that she had somehow missed. When she moved them a second time downstairs into the basement, she again sought a missing offspring, calling for him to come out of his hiding place. Then she would move them a third time, back up the cellar stairs into my bedroom on the first floor. On each occasion a day or two passed before she got over her loss.

She was a diligent mother. I can still see her, firmly pinning down a struggling kitten with her forepaw and subjecting him to a thorough washing with her rough tongue. The kittens did not object but soon scampered off, slightly damp, but whistle clean. As they grew and learned to drink from a saucer, Happy's worries grew with them. She wanted her kittens to be with her in her box, cuddled up and clinging to her, sucking away on her nipples. She was, in short, the eternal mother, human or feline, who never wants her progeny to leave the nest. Alas, she soon found herself roaming the house, uttering that special mother-cat cry, a distinct throaty plaint that differed from the "Hey, let me in!" howl or the querulous "Where's the grub?" plea, or the low gurgle of a mew that signals "I'm jumping on your bed, please welcome me."

In the hot summer days I moved out of my room and into the deserted garage that came with the property. In those days, only the privileged owned a car and thus we had space to burn. Happy joined me in the garage; for once, she could keep an eye on her kittens. Alas, for her, they refused to be corralled, dashing about, evading her clutches, chasing their tails, rolling on and off my bed until, exhausted, they suddenly dropped wherever they were. Thus, in the light of dawn, the garage floor seemed to be covered with a living carpet.

They were clean kittens. Happy had seen to that. When nature called, they let me know. I remember one kitten we called Pieface after a popular candy bar—the litter were all named after confections that season—who jumped up on the bed and poked me in the face with an open paw until I did his bidding and let him out.

When Happy wanted to go out she sat quietly beside the garage door until I rose and opened it. No fuss, no howls; she simply gave me the tabby cat stare and I obeyed. But there was one mystery. How did she get back in? Out she'd go, the door would slam, but by morning there she was back inside, sleeping on my bed. It was the kind of illusion that stage magicians, like Blackstone, were showing off in the Capitol Theatre on Yates Street. *A cat who seemed able to walk through walls!* How did she pull that off?

I discovered her secret early one morning after I'd put her out. A sudden rattling on the wall above me, a scratching sound, and suddenly "Plop!" as in the funny papers, and Happy landed on my bed. She had managed to leap up and claw her way into the space between the wall and the sloping roof, squeeze through it, and presto! she was back inside. One or two of her kittens tried it—Pieface especially—with lamentable results. They'd fling themselves at the outside wall and then topple back, unable to reach the roof.

The cat endured. We moved from Victoria to Vancouver. My father returned from the North. I went off to war, came back, married, and left for the East; but the cat remained as much a part of the household as the Persian rug—Potty's nemesis—which had followed the family from the Yukon. As the family cat, she enjoyed certain privileges or, rather, took them on herself. When my sister, Lucy, returned from work of an evening, Happy would wait for her, hidden in the branches of the big-leaved catalpa tree down the street. As Lucy passed under the tree, Happy would jump on her shoulder and hitch a ride to the front door.

She continued to churn out kittens—far too many for my mother to handle, especially with my father ill and in the hospital. The Depression was over but its memory lingered. Tinned cat food was unknown. There were no expensive visits to the vet. It did not occur to my mother to have Happy spayed. Instead she simply drowned the kittens as soon as they were born. She managed it as humanely as she could, filling a large bucket with warm water, putting each one-day-old kitten in a sock weighted with stones and dropping them, one after another, into the bucket. Sometimes she would keep one alive to soothe the lactating mother's discomfort. But on one memorable occasion, she drowned all four.

She told me about the experience with considerable awe after I returned from overseas and from training camp in Brandon to attend my father's funeral. It is a remarkable tale, but I have no reason to doubt it, even though she was a journalist's daughter and writer herself who understood the old bromide about never letting the truth get in the way of a good story. This was certainly a good story, but I don't believe my mother made it up.

She had drowned all four kittens, she told me, and had taken the little bodies out of their socks and placed them in a shallow grave scooped out in the kitchen garden. After covering them with a shovelful or two of loam she left to go shopping.

When she returned and walked into her kitchen, she couldn't believe her eyes. There was Happy, lying on her side, eyes closed in ecstasy, with a tiny blind morsel of a kitten firmly fastened to each nipple.

At first my mother thought these must be strange kittens, retrieved from another mother; but that was preposterous. A closer look convinced her that these indeed were Happy's tiny offspring—the ones she had drowned and buried less than two hours before.

There was no doubt about it. Happy had gone out to the garden, clawed away at the earth, retrieved her kittens, breathed new life into them and carried each one through the cellar door and up the stairs to the kitchen. She had washed the dirt off each and nursed them back to health. She looked up at my astonished parent and uttered a rare mew, as if to say, in her triumph, "Don't try it again!" Nor did my mother have the heart to go through the whole fruitless exercise a second time.

 ## SEBASTIAN: THE SANTA CLAUS CAT

Happy had switched her allegiance to my mother, who, after all, was the one who fed her after I married and moved out of the house. Inevitably, cats are faithful not to their masters and mistresses, but to hearth and home—to that small corner of the kitchen or basement where a saucer of milk awaits them, to that cozy wing chair where they can doze, protected against nameless enemies. The newspapers have always featured tales of cats (like Pousse-Pousse) who have managed to find their way home, even to a new city and sometimes to a new country. It is the hearth that lures them back.

We hear a good deal about one-man dogs, the kind who refuse to be torn from their master's corpse after his death. But one-man cats? The phrase is not part of the language. Cat owners spend a great deal of time and ingenuity trying to figure out distinctive names for their pets—like Felix, Spooky, and Esmerelda, who once scampered through the comic pages. But the cats don't give a hoot. If you call to your dog: "Here Spot! Here, boy!" Spot comes trotting over, tongue hanging out, eyes alight, because he recognizes his name. Cats know the language too, but they put a different spin on it. You may think that "Kitty" as in "Here, Kitty, Kitty!" or "Moonbeam" as in "Here, Moonbeam, here Moonbeam!" are invitations that bring the cats rushing into your arms. Forget it! It brings them rushing for the vittles.

When we first married, our tiny bachelor flat (all we could get in that era of housing shortages) wasn't big enough for any kind of pet. When we moved to Toronto and sublet a one-bedroom walk-up on an inside court we were even more crowded. But when we moved again to a one-room flat above a hardware store in East York, we started to search about for a cat—any cat—that was free to a good home. We found what we wanted in Oakville during a visit to my Uncle Phil, who wrote a regular column for the local paper and knew enough people with mother cats to allow us a choice of kittens. We selected a newly weaned black-and-white kitty and brought him home by bus and street-car, a small ball of fluff who nestled in my wife's coat and merci-fully fell asleep for the entire trip. We named him Sebastian.

We had another visitor that month, our friend Himie Koshevoy, the puckish city editor of my old paper, *The Vancouver Sun*. As he and I sat in our tiny front room, sipping Hudson's Bay rum and watching the kitten carom off the walls, the subject nat-urally turned to journalism and the roles cats play in headlines.

"Wherever there's a fire and someone's house burns down, you'll always find a cat," Himie was saying. "They are essential to any good fire story, even if you have to go out and drag one in." He was right, of course. Every month or so the papers carry a headline about a cat saving people from a blazing building.

And, as Himie noted, the headline is always just about the same: HERO CAT SAVES TWELVE IN MYSTERY BLAZE

"Come on, do you really think cats save people in fires?" I asked him.

"It's what you call a moot point," Himie said. "The evidence is hazy. A big fire takes place, every reporter is looking for an angle. It helps a lot if you can find a cat somewhere who has very sensibly left the building."

In those days in Toronto, with three aggressive newspapers all battling each other, every reporter was looking for a scoop. Competition was fierce and the cat angle.

"If the cat doesn't leave the building," he said, "then you have another exclusive story about how a brave child rushed back into the flames to haul her favourite pet to safety. Picture of building, picture of child, picture of a cat—all on page one. Big newsstand sales to cat lovers."

I agreed: "But, of course, there's always some damn dog in the way, hungry for headlines. You know, 'the faithful canine' angle."

"Cats make bigger headlines," Himie said. "After all, you expect dogs to do their duty. But cats generally stand aloof. You know that. So when one breaks the pattern, or more properly, is *reported* to have broken the pattern, that's news."

"Remember the cat that looked like Hitler," I said.

"Sure do. You and Filion used that animal as an excuse to get out of the office."

He was right. Harry Filion, my closest friend, was the *Sun*'s chief photographer, and we liked working together—me writing the copy and Harry providing the pictures. It was our habit each afternoon, when the Home edition had been put to bed, to drive around town looking for something to happen while we consumed a mickey of cheap rye.

When Janet told me that there was a cat living in her hometown who was known to resemble the late German führer, we had our excuse for a day in the country free of the usual newsroom constraints.

We drove off to Haney, a small community in the Fraser Valley, checked in at Walker's Store (presided over by my father-in-law), and after a few discreet inquiries, found the cat. There he was, just as advertised, a white shorthair, with black hair on his forehead and a small black moustache. When I raised his paw in a familiar salute, Harry snapped the picture.

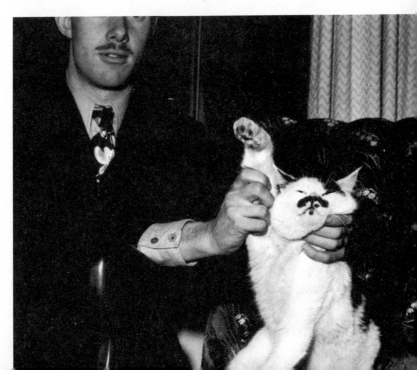

"It wasn't much of a picture," Himie said. "Didn't *really* look like Hitler."

"Well, you put it on the front page."

"No. Front page of the City section. It was a slow news day. And after all, you wrote the caption."

"A lot of subscribers got a kick out of it."

"Cat lovers," he said. "A special breed. Not like dog lovers. Cat lovers like pictures of cats—*any* cat. That's why we ran the photo. But a dog lover is only interested in one specific breed—*his*. Incidentally, did you ever see a dog that looked like Hitler?"

"Now that cat," Himie said, pointing his finger at Sebastian, who was starting to guzzle a saucer of milk, "that cat isn't a special breed; that cat is a mongrel but cat lovers don't care." He reached down and tickled the kitten who, between mouthfuls of milk, began to purr.

"It's not fair that we should be sitting here carousing without including the kitty," Himie said, as he poured a little rum into the saucer.

Sebastian lapped it up greedily.

"Hey, not so fast," said Himie; but it was too late. The kitten had polished it off.

"Now you've got him pickled," I said, as Sebastian looked up a little blearily, then sat down suddenly.

"Join the party," Himie said, reaching for the kitten. But Sebastian had managed to struggle to his feet and was now trying to make his way across the room. He made it halfway across, then toppled over on his nose and remained in that position, bottom up. We let him sleep it off.

Was this brief encounter with the bottle the reason why Sebastian, in his many years with us, had no kittens? For *he* was a *she*, as we soon discovered, and a barren one. We changed her name to Sebastienne, but she produced no progeny.

Two years later, when we moved into our newly built house in the country, Sebastienne moved with us. Hopeful toms came to visit her, but she remained kittenless. She liked the country as much as we did, and being a clean cat, always asked permission to go outside.

But how did she get back into the house? We would put her out at night, lock all the doors, close the windows tight, and go to bed. The following morning, there she would be in her basket purring contentedly.

Sebastian, the gender-bender kitten

Somehow, like Happy, she had figured out a foolproof method of re-entry. But how? There was no gap between roof and wall for her to squeeze through as there was in Happy's time.

Months went by before we twigged. One winter's night after a party, when all our city friends were gone and Janet and our two small daughters were safely in bed, Farley Mowat, the last of our guests, and I sat in the living room, trying our best to demolish a bottle of rum. Our excuse was that Mowat needed the rum to thaw out. I had found him in the driveway, snoring away in the front seat of his pickup, long after the party-goers had departed. He was chilled to the marrow and obviously in need of first aid. So there we were, warming ourselves in front of the big stone fireplace, when suddenly, a black apparition appeared out of the smoke and embers in a shower of sparks, leaped down to the floor and dashed off to the kitchen.

I was as shaken as he was. It was, to put it mildly, a sobering experience. But there, in the corner of the kitchen where the cat food was always kept, was Sebastienne, carefully licking the ashes off her fur.

Another cat mystery solved! And one that would pay dividends in the future, livening up otherwise uneventful evenings as the cat made her unexpected entry down the chimney. The fireplace is massive, fashioned out of Credit Valley limestone, with a corner hearth situated a foot-and-a-half above the floor. The ingenious cat, desperate to come in out of the cold, had managed to claw her way up to the roof, climb into the chimney and plunge to the hearth, landing on all fours and making her escape before she was so much as singed.

There was no way we could dissuade her in this mad enterprise. She loved the chimney, because, like all cats, she loved a warm spot. I soon discovered that when the fire was out, she liked to crouch on the smoke ledge halfway up the chimney's interior. I must admit, a little sheepishly, that I encouraged her, because she was the life of the party on those evenings when she made her explosive entrance. Women screamed; strong men turned pale. The cat, oblivious to the sensation she was causing, was soon curled up in her corner by the fireplace, studiously washing her face.

There were other satisfying moments in the summer when the grate was cold. It was my habit to ply a visitor with a couple of after-dinner cognacs before turning his attention to the fireplace. "Take a look up the chimney," I'd suggest. "It's worth examining the workmanship." The mark would peer up into the gloom and then let out a cry at the sight of two unblinking yellow eyes staring down at him. The devil himself could not have produced a more satisfying reaction.

No one was more baffled by the chimney cat than my two little girls, both under the age of six. Sebastienne's unorthodox arrival played hell with the Santa Claus myth. Was the jolly old elf really a cat? Or was Sebastienne simply Santa in disguise? One Christmas Eve we put out the requisite milk and cookies to speed him and his reindeer on their way. The cat promptly came down the chimney and gobbled up the yuletide offering.

Sebastienne in her later years

THREE

Hobo Cats

PUNKOO AND MARMALADE

There are times when I am convinced that there are cabalistic cat scratches on our front door resembling the scribbled code left by hobos during the Depression years. When deciphered by other cats these messages translate to: *Free Board and Lodging Inside.* How else to account for the long feline procession that has sought us out, moved in, and stayed seemingly forever?

This doesn't happen with our neighbours. Stray cats do not seek them out, nor do frustrated cat owners negotiate their driveways and leave boxes of kittens on their doorsteps. My memories of the days that followed the arrival of Sebastienne are hazy now, but I cannot forget the face of the tawny cat that appeared at our bedroom window one rainy winter's night, staring straight into our eyes and howling like a banshee until we let her in.

Her? Yellow cats are almost always male. But this was definitely a lady cat and an expectant mother at that, dripping wet. She went straight to our clothes closet and next morning I found four kittens in my shoes. We called her Pumpkin, for that was her colour, but to the children, who could not pronounce the word, she was always Punkoo.

Punkoo was one smart cat. My mother was visiting us at the time; undeterred by memories of Happy, the gravedigger, she prepared immediately to polish off the progeny. Punkoo was too fast for her; the kittens all vanished and did not reappear until they were four weeks old and far too cute to be put down.

Even more astonishing was the appearance of another yellow (or at least partially yellow) cat at the same window one year later and again in a driving rainstorm. Of course we let her in and of course she too had kittens in my clothes closet. And again, like Punkoo, Marmalade proceeded next day to hide her offspring.

What the hell is going on here? I asked Janet. Two yellow pussycats arrive at our window under similar circumstances and—in spite of the odds against yellow females—they each have kittens and in the same place. Is there a kind of mental telepathy among yellow cats?

The similarities are spooky. Marmalade too hid her kittens and we couldn't find them. But where? Well, we did have a shed crammed with every kind of discarded junk: cardboard boxes full of old magazines and newspapers that my wife thought might be useful for the children's school essays; pop bottles that had never been returned and some that would never be returnable; worn-out shirts, shoes, and other articles of apparel that were supposed to be sent off to the Crippled Civilians, who collected such items for resale; shovels and rakes with broken handles awaiting repairs that would never be made; clay pots full of special potting soil presented to us with a package of nasturtium seeds or a few roots of African violets; a clock that needed fixing; a coil of partially unravelled rope; several tins of insecticides that the newspapers warned us never to use; a broken tricycle; two worn-out rubber tires—need I go on? My wife is a squirrel, a child of the Depression who cannot bear to throw anything out, be it a discarded silver slipper or four years' supply of the *National Geographic*, unread. Or, I might add, a stray cat.

In this exotic labyrinth, the four little kittens, fed by their cunning mother, flourished and gambolled, safe from the storm, not to mention marauding grandmothers. And this had happened *twice.* The first time we half-believed they had been gobbled up by a predator in the forest. The next time we knew better. There was Marmalade, calmly licking her chops by her saucer in the kitchen corner, then sauntering off into the night with her nipples the size of thumbs. And there, four weeks later, was this gaggle of pussycats—black, yellow, white, and beige— bouncing about the house and scoffing down tins of Dr. Ballard's most expensive gourmet cat food.

Looking back today I can view the struggle that went on between the various mother cats and my own mother with equanimity. I do not wish here to depict my parent as a wicked kitten killer; she was anything but. She was simply determined to reduce the cat population in our home—and indeed the world—to a manageable number.

Most mother cats seem capable of producing at least three litters a year. As my mother pointed out, three mother cats could produce as many as fifty kittens in a twelve-month period. Let them, by all means, have their fun with the tattered toms who haunted the back fences of the nation, but be ruthless with the resulting issue. Otherwise we would be up to our buttocks in cats, as indeed certain dear old ladies are, if we are to believe the newspaper stories.

It was an uneven struggle, but occasionally the mother cat won, as Happy the gravedigger had won, and as Punkoo and Marmalade had won. As they both sensed, it is one thing to euthanize a one-day-old kitten; it is quite another to execute a lively, blue-eyed bundle of fluff. My mother, who was in her eighties at the time, had no stomach for it and neither did we, which explains why our home in Kleinburg always seemed to be crawling with felines of various breeds and ages.

 PYRAMUS AND THISBE

To our growing cat population was now added an additional pair who simply turned up on our doorstep one morning in a cardboard box left by someone who had, apparently, driven down our long driveway without detection, or maybe walked, lugging the box of cats with them. They were clearly from the same litter and had reached an undrownable age, both black with white shirtwaists and the standard winsome faces. Somebody in our growing family was studying *A Midsummer Night's Dream* at school, and as a result, the two kittens acquired the names of Pyramus and Thisbe, after the play within the play.

Thisbe began having kittens as soon as she reached puberty. My mother, who was again present at the birth, immediately drowned all four before they could be spirited away. Thisbe, however, outwitted her. The following day, with her newborn children in their graves, she strode into the hall closet and produced a *fifth* kitten. What could we do? My mother went along with this last-minute reprieve, and the cat population at our house increased by one more.

Pyramus, meanwhile, had been conducting a flirtation with our dog, Gerry, who was half collie and half mutt. To say that Gerry was a friendly dog does not do justice to the slobbering affection that he showered on all of us, including little Pyramus. As a watchdog he was a bust. Like all our future collies—five in all—he would have been the first to lead any burglar directly to the swag. Now he lavished his affection on the black kitten, licking him down with his soft tongue as if he was his mother. Pyramus replied by snuggling up to Gerry and purring loudly. Most of the time Gerry liked to lick Pyramus's ears; and that brings me to another bizarre episode—unbelievable, but true—in this checkered anthology of true cat tales. *Gerry licked the kitten's ears off.* And the kitten encouraged the slow amputation!

Gerry didn't do it all at once, but in stages and with the cat's enthusiastic agreement. The ears kept getting ragged and then smaller and smaller. For some weeks Pyramus walked about with Band-Aids covering his ears; but Gerry kept licking and he kept purring, and one day Pyramus was earless.

I was writing a kid's novel at the time, starring five of my offspring, including our newborn son, Paul, whom the children called Pollywog. In the novel, *The Secret World of Og*, I gave each of my characters pets; and since the characters of the children in the book were based on those of real children—my own—why not give them real pets in the story?

Gerry, our collie, appears in the book in the guise of Yukon King, a little dog who thinks he's a big dog like the one on television. Pyramus became Earless Osdick. The name was a play on words. At the time Al Capp's comic strip, *L'il Abner*, was a huge favourite. Abner's "ideal" was Fearless Fosdick, a spoof of the popular *Dick Tracy* strip. It was an inside joke of course and not one many six year olds would catch. But I also wrote the book for fathers, like me, who were fed up with the Spot-and-Puff stories and needed a few jokes for themselves.

But because my audience was mainly composed of small children, I decided to soften the bit about the ears. In my story, the cat wasn't really earless, he just liked to wear his ears folded down like a dog. Here is the relevant passage:

> *Though pretending to eat his Pablum, the Pollywog*
> *was really feeding it to Earless Osdick, the black cat*
> *who sat directly below the high chair. Earless Osdick*
> *was the Pollywog's inseparable companion. Grown-ups*
> *used to say to each other: "Isn't it touching how the cat*
> *follows that child everywhere he goes?" This simply*
> *proves they didn't know much about cats. The reason*
> *Earless Osdick followed the Pollywog everywhere and*

sat so faithfully beneath the high chair was because the Pollywog fed him constantly. Sometimes the Pollywog did it on purpose and sometimes he did it because he wasn't very good at eating. He would miss with his spoon and Earless Osdick would lap up the Pablum as it fell. Earless Osdick loved Pablum. As for the Pollywog, he liked Earless Osdick to sit under the high chair because on those occasions when he did escape, he landed on him and the cat cushioned his fall.

That was more or less true. But how could I explain the earless aspect of the cat without making it seem too grisly? The solution, when I arrived at it, actually improved the story:

When Earless Osdick was a kitten, he had been brought up with the dog, whose name was Yukon King. He was called Earless Osdick because he kept his ears folded down like a dog, and not sharply upright like a cat. This is because he slept with the dog, ate with the dog, and thought he was a dog. He and Yukon King tried barking daily, without much success, but they still kept at it.

Thus did Pyramus, acting as a stand-in for a fictional cat, help me create a new and memorable character in what was to become my biggest-selling book. I used him again in Chapter Nine: "Earless Osdick's Secret Mission," and when I finished writing it I poured him a saucer of pure cream. "I couldn't have done it without you," I told him.

THE TRANSFIGURATION OF FLUFFY

About this time we had another visitor, a beautiful white Persian named Fluffy. She belonged to the people in the house across the road, but she spent half her time at our place, sleeping on Pamela's bed, chowing down on whatever was available, and lying stretched out on the chesterfield, like a pampered cat in a Hollywood film.

Then, one day, she encountered another visitor—the puckish, Hungarian-born cartoonist George Feyer, whose cartoons appeared regularly in *Maclean's* and *Collier's*. George was certainly the fastest cartoonist in the world, a talent he later honed on CBC Television. The felt pen was his instrument and it helped make George the master of his medium. George gazed down upon Fluffy, taking her ease on our sofa, and Fluffy gazed back at him. In that instant, a new art form was born.

George was congenitally unable to ignore any white space on which he might exercise his talents. He drew on everything; on bare walls in our children's rooms and sometimes on the children themselves. He drew elephants with big ears on the bare bodies on my two little boys, using their appendages as trunks— an ingenious bit of artistry that they both refused to erase, thus reducing their pediatrician to a state of helpless hilarity.

When George gazed upon Fluffy, he didn't see a cat, he saw an empty canvas. Out came the ubiquitous felt pen, and Fluffy acquired an instant mustache. A black beret, worn rakishly over one eye, followed. George warmed to his work. He added a bow-tie at Fluffy's neck and then the semblance of a tuxedo. He gave her red-striped socks, a tiger's tail, and, as a final flourish, covered her torso with blue and red spots. Fluffy didn't care; her attitude was "anything for a free meal." She yawned, stretched, padded off down our driveway, made it across the road, and entered her home suitably disguised.

I will draw a veil over the aftermath. Her owners had been immodestly proud of Fluffy, and a little patronizing—stressing the fact that she was a pure-bred Persian, unlike the raffish lower-class cats who found their way to our door. Now they hit the roof. You'd have thought that we had murdered their cat, not decorated her. Janet did her best to placate them with a bottle of rye while I tried to make amends by suffering through one of their marathon evenings of home movies; horses aplenty in the innumerable reels of their trip to the Rockies. But, alas, not a single cat.

FOUR

Survivor Cats

I AM A SUCKER FOR TABBY CATS, PARTLY BECAUSE OF HAPPY, but also because tabbies are survivors. I admire them. They are smarter than many of the beautiful show cats who have had the brains bred out of them. They carry, beneath their stripes, an agglomeration of genes that prepare them for the vicissitudes of cat existence. Give me a mongrel cat any day, I say!

I am thinking of my two-year-old son, Peter, and the kitten, a tabby of course, who clung to him, not through thick and thin, but through mud and water. Peter was two at the time, an adventurous child who, one day, simply disappeared from our home. No sign of him! You can imagine the hue and cry. Neighbours forming posses, plunging into the forest, preparing to drag the river, searching the byways. No Peter—and, though nobody noticed, no kitten.

Peter, of course, was not lost; we were. He was happily trudging off down the road, kitten in hand, enjoying his freedom. The problem was that he was faster than anybody could imagine. We looked and we looked but the search circle was never wide enough. At last a passing motorist told us he'd seen a small boy with a damp kitten strolling along Teston Road about a half mile from our home. We'd never expected him to wander that far.

So there he was, our collie dog with him, holding the kitten by the neck and dunking it like a doughnut in every muddy pond along the way. People rushed to make sure the boy was all right, and of course he was mystified by all the fuss. Nobody bothered about the little cat.

I was concerned for the health of the kitten, who was soaking wet, shivering, and obviously half drowned. Remembering Sebastian, I poured him a saucer of rum and milk, which he gobbled greedily. I wrapped him in a hot towel. He survived, and so of course, did Peter. Small boys and kittens really do need to be kept on a leash.

 ## WALLY SIMPSON AND HAMILTON BEACH

It is exceedingly rare for any cat to live past his second decade. At the age of twenty he is in the same bracket as an eighty-year-old human. I suspect that Wally Simpson, our male tabby, holds some kind of record for surviving the millennium at the age of twenty-four. I have the documents to prove it. I found him in a tree in 1976, the year Mao Zedong, a fellow oldster, passed on. I know that because the chairman's death robbed Wally of his fifteen minutes of fame. *Maclean's* magazine was reviewing a book of mine that week and had planned a feature story and cover. The cover, which showed me, my book, and the kitten in my arms, was ready to roll off the presses. But *Maclean's* was now a newsmagazine, and Mao pushed me and

Wally out of the limelight. So he was a kitten in 1976, right? And the last veterinarian bill is clearly dated 1999. He made it into 2000, but there are no further bills. He was a tough old cat, but he couldn't live forever.

He was, of course, a tabby. I heard his cries echoing all over our nine acres and finally came upon him, a tiny morsel of grey and white caught in the upper branches of a weeping willow

Cover of Maclean's *with me and little Wally*

next to the road. I remembered earlier that day passing a little girl sitting by the road beneath the tree playing with a cat. Now I realized, not without a pang of sympathy, that she was saying good-bye to her kitten, undoubtedly at the insistence of her parents. I wonder if she remembers that scene after a quarter of a century? If she does and she reads this, I hope she will be reassured that her little cat led a wonderful life in the country; a mighty hunter who often foraged for his own wild food, who never complained, lived for twenty-four years, and remained cheerful to the end.

The second-oldest cat in our menagerie was Wally Simpson's friend and companion, a brown and black longhair called Hamilton Beach, who had a purr as rasping as a mixer. He was really Patsy's cat but she brought him out to Kleinburg "for his summer holidays," as she put it. He liked the country so much, he never left. He lived into his late teens and, even in their winter years, he and Wally Simpson would play together, jumping on each other like kittens and engaging in a chase down our hall.

Unlike Wally, a straight-ahead tabby who had no personal idiosyncrasies, Hamilton Beach was a bundle of weird neuroses. He was so nutty that I wrote asking for the advice of two of the cat columnists who appeared regularly in the press, Dr. Anne Huntington and Dr. Paul McCutcheon.

Here is what I wrote:

"My cat, Hamilton Beach, needs help. He is a male
Persian, fixed, of indeterminate years, probably about 9
or 10, and is named for his distinctive purr, which
sounds like a mixing machine gone slightly wonky.
We are not sure of his age because we don't know
his birthday, having got him from a local farmer.
Unfortunately, like most people brought up in a barn,
his habits are a little strange. And that's why I'm
writing to you.

"You have heard that old cliché: 'Look what the
cat dragged in?' Well, that is the crux of the problem.
The Beach, as we call him, was a great mouser in his
younger days. But one day, he stopped going after mice.
Instead, he began to drag things into our bedroom,
scarves, old socks, pantyhose, underwear, even bath
towels. We could hear him as he moved slowly down
the hall toward the bedroom, occasionally leaping on
his prey and gnawing at it.

"It's grown worse. It occurs mostly in the evenings.
In the morning, the bedroom and the hallway are lit-
tered with garments of various descriptions.

"So, is Hamilton Beach completely bonkers?" Are
you familiar with this syndrome?"

Dr. Huntington was good enough to reply as follows:

"I must confess, that in all of my long experience I have never heard or seen the kind of behavior you note in your letter."

Never? Really? Never? Wow! I own a unique cat!

"I'm wondering how you treated him the days when he caught a mouse," Dr. Huntington asked. "Did you laugh at him?"

Laugh at my cat? Perish the thought.

"Or did you praise him as a mighty hunter? That could have affected his psyche. This is obviously transference behaviour," Dr. H. opined, "but I've never encountered it before. He seems to have become a clothing fetishist. Certainly he seems to be using these objects—socks, lingerie, etc., as surrogate mice."

Dr. McCutcheon followed in a similar vein:

"There is little doubt that Hamilton Beach is suffering from an identity crisis. The clothing he is presenting you with in all likelihood is a surrogate mouse. But the real question is why does he feel the need to do this?

"Presenting you with mice was fulfilling his natural instincts as a provider His innate instincts were to be putting bread on the table for his family (of which

*you are prime members). Mice aren't so easy to get as
they used to be. He is getting a little older and the mice
seem to be getting a little faster! The clothing, on the
other hand, is easy prey; the fact that it is inedible is
not an issue anyway so why not concentrate on what
he can do efficiently instead of being frustrated with his
declining capabilities?*

*"To avoid the nightly clothing attack, why not
provide Hamilton Beach with a better surrogate, a
mouse toy, say? When he presents you with the mouse,
demonstrate your approval, lots of petting, perhaps
some favourite treat. Show him that you appreciate his
efforts. With a little psychological retraining you will be
giving him the feeling of fulfillment that he seems to
need, while avoiding the clothing ritual you don't need."*

I showed both these expert responses to Peggy Anne, who
grew up with Hamilton Beach. She looked at me oddly "Dad,"
she said "it's not a surrogate mouse the cat is toying with; it's a
surrogate cat."

Really? "Yes, really. The cat is sex mad. He's not just drag-
ging in scarves and socks: he's humping them. Haven't you
noticed?"

I'm shocked. My cat, a sex pervert?

"Take a look. There are obvious physical signs."

"But ... that cat has been fixed."

"Sure but did you ever tell that to the cat?"

FIVE

The Siamese Imperative

THE CATS OF POTTERY ROAD

Siamese cat lovers, like their expensive pets, are a world apart. They dismiss the impassive tabby as a lesser species and prose-lytize with great fervour for the royal cats of Siam. The pressure is constant and that helps to explain why I succumbed. I did not plan to own a Siamese but at least, I thought, I could write about the craze that was sweeping the country.

I had been told by more than one Siamese addict that somewhere in the upper Don Valley, in a 120-year-old house of mud brick, there lived a woman who had a company of thirty Siamese cats. So I drove north along Broadview, which used to be Mill Road, turned down the old trail known as Pottery Road, and into that most ancient of suburbs that a century ago was known as The Circle of the Don.

There, among the elms and willows, far from the jungle of the city, lay a little pool of history. The world seemed a hundred miles away. One house dated back to the eighteenth century; it had no fewer than five fireplaces. Its neighbour, a great square edifice, had walls that were eighteen inches thick.

I knocked on the door of that house and presently a pretty little woman wearing a printed smock covered with pictures of cats ushered me inside. This was Marjorie Elliott, who had helped start the Canadian Siamese cat craze.

"I come from a long line of cat lovers," she explained, and as I entered, a white ball on the couch detached itself into three separate and sinuous shapes. They flowed onto the floor and glided around our legs like serpents. The effect was at once eerie and intriguing, for each seemed to be wearing a Halloween mask of richest brown with pointed ears to match.

"When I first saw a Siamese cat after the war, I simply had to have one and *that* was that!" Mrs. Elliott told me. As she spoke I saw two more of these ghostly animals perched on a space heater, staring down at us like birds of prey. This was a new experience for me. These strange cats bore little resemblance to Pyramus, Happy, or Sebastienne.

"A few years ago there was hardly one of these cats in Canada," Mrs. Elliott explained. "Down Zhabo! But now three-quarters of the cats on show are Siamese."

She led the way into a second room, a veritable swarm of cats. The door had scarcely closed before one reached my shoulder in a single leap, purring throatily.

"I'm afraid Holly is a little too friendly," Mrs. Elliott murmured, as she poked her finger into a writhing basket of chalk-white kittens. "These cats were unknown in the western world until 1866. They were the royal cats of Siam and jealously guarded, but the British consul-general in Bangkok brought two to Britain that year and I'd say most of these cats are descended from that pair."

Three cats appeared from nowhere and arranged themselves like table decorations in a perfect circle. Two more appeared and adopted grave, statuesque positions by the door. I felt eyes watching me and, turning, came face to face with the loveliest female I had ever seen, with ears of soft grey-blue, feet to match, and mild deep-blue eyes.

"That's Moonbeam of Chen Ling," said Mrs. Elliott. "The blues are softer in every way than the seals, but the seals are more vital."

I was now being given a course on Siamese Cats 101. Where these mysterious animals originally came from no one knows. The original Royal Siamese were sealpoint, their bodies creamy white, their extremities a rich brown. But mutant strains have produced the delicate bluepoints, the chocolatepoints, the frostpoints, the lilacpoints, and more recently, the redpoints, with orange ears and tails.

"Come in and meet the boys," said Mrs. Elliott as we entered a third room full of proud males pacing restlessly in their cages. The other cats all trooped in silently behind us, carefully adopting decorative positions. I thought of Sebastienne, legging it across the floor after a trip down the chimney; yes, these cats *were* different.

"Roll over for the man, Shan-dur," said Mrs. Elliott, and a big bluepoint obediently turned turtle. I made to stroke him but he gave me a fierce look and went over to a corner of the cage to sulk.

"Shan-dur hates men," Mrs. Elliott explained. "Come on, Shan-dur, roll over again."

But the cat stubbornly refused. Instead, a cat in a neighbouring cage rolled over agreeably.

"Smartest cats in the world," Mrs. Elliott told me. "Some of mine even try to answer the telephone. They're better than dogs."

I took out my sketch book and, back in the living room, began to sketch the cats. One came up, stared into my face, and emitted a single, husky howl. Another leaped into my lap and tried to steal my pencil.

"Siamese cats hate to be ignored," said Mrs. Elliott. "Oh, dear! I'm afraid Zhabo and Saladin have made a nest out of your hat!"

I retrieved it, pocketed my sketch book, and took my leave. Outside, in the ancient Circle of the Don, the world seemed ghostly quiet—quieter even than in those early days when men brewed beer here and fashioned pots of clay, and ground wheat to flour, and knew nothing at all about the royal cats who lived secretly in an Oriental palace hidden from the view of ordinary mortals. I did not turn my head but could almost feel the thirty-odd pairs of inquisitive blue eyes, staring through the eighteen-inch mud walls, and boring into my back as I walked away toward civilization.

SARI

Of course I surrendered to the Siamese cat craze. A week later I was back at Mrs. Elliott's, purchasing a tiny bluepoint female kitten with the pretentious name of Shen-Ling Sari. She quickly grew up and proceeded to produce kittens at an alarming rate. A couple of years later she had her fifteen minutes of fame when I decided to take her along on a family houseboat trip down Ontario's twisting Trent-Severn Canal. This 240-mile lake-and-river system stretches from Port Severn on Georgian Bay to Trenton on Lake Ontario. Sari, having just mothered another batch of kittens, deserved an outing.

Off we went: Janet, two sons and four daughters, including the six-week-old baby, Peggy Anne, *plus* the Princess Sari (as I dubbed her in print) and one of her kittens—a last-minute addition. We had planned to sell him before the voyage began, but hadn't got around to it, so we brought him along to keep his mother company. The children had named all the kittens in Sari's litter after condiments and spices such as Mustard, Ginger, and Paprika, to distinguish them from the kittens of another litter named for herbs: Parsley, Sage, Rosemary, Thyme, and Newsweek (the latter an outrageous pun for which I take full responsibility).

In the interests of journalism, I gave the new kitten a more distinguished name. In my articles written during the houseboat trip, I referred to him as Prince Paprika of Kowloon. His mother worried constantly, prowling the boat's railings and mewing when he threatened to jump overboard, which, of course, he did. We pulled him bedraggled from Lake Couchiching. His mother tongue-dried him from ear to tail, and from then on he behaved himself.

She continued to be half-baffled, half bemused by the voyage, sitting out on the roof of the cabin from which she sometimes had to be forcibly dislodged.

At night, when we lay moored against the dark banks, she stared through the windows with her Oriental eyes and howled at strange things in the forest. What did she see back there in the gloom? We could not tell, but whatever they were, they were very real to her and also, I suspect to the smaller children. Perhaps, I suggested, they were the ghosts of native warriors; after all, this was the best known warpath in all Canada.

We chugged across Lake Couchiching in a high wind and paused at Big Chief Island to let everybody, including the cats, stretch their legs. Here Sari escaped into the forest, moving as swiftly as any fleeing Huron while her kitten struggled in Pamela's arms. By the time we pushed off again, the wind had risen, blowing from the northwest, and the boat, caught in the trough between the waves, rolled wickedly, tossing the small children off their bunks and bringing a flood of lake water under the door to the galley. It was only when we docked at Orillia—Stephen Leacock's hometown—that we realized Princess Sari was missing.

Everybody remembered her scampering off into the forest, but none could recall seeing her return. And nobody had given her absence much thought as the wind rose and the waves lashed the shore. It was clear that someone would have to go back to Big Chief Island to rescue the abandoned cat, not in the big, ungainly houseboat, but in a smaller craft. A fellow mariner at the dock offered his services and Janet volunteered to make the trip with him. But how would she find Sari? The

OPPOSITE: *Sari on the roof being teased down with a big net*

island was large, as its name suggests—a jungle of conifers and underbrush near the centre of the storm-swept lake. It was now pouring rain. What to do?

The only possibility, Janet said, was to take Paprika along for the ride in the hopes that his cries would lure his mother from the bushes. With the kitten hidden under Janet's slicker, they pushed off through the rain. The island was hidden by the wind-driven spray, but at last Janet was able to make out the shoreline lying low in the choppy waters. She peered into the murk and, as the boat approached the beach, she fumbled to reach Paprika and to prod him into full voice. Then, just before the boat touched the shore, she made out her quarry. There was

Patsy with
Princess Sari

Sari, waiting at the water's edge, totally unconcerned, standing tall, Siamese-fashion. As the boat touched the shore she leaped aboard and proceeded to wash Paprika down. Janet admired her confidence and her composure. Sari had been sure we would come back for her.

Two days later, by the time the canal system took us through Fenelon Falls, Sari had become a famous cat. As we passed under the bridge a huge crowd, clinging to the rails, shouted down to us. "Show us the cat!" they cried, and we hoisted her up for all to see. This brief moment of fame, sparked by my newspaper column, did not turn her head. She gratefully acknowledged the onlookers from her perch in Pamela's arms, then dropped to the deck to corral her frisky kitten and lick him all over for the umpteenth time that day.

 WHISPER

She was the most prolific cat we ever owned, a bluepoint from Mrs. Elliott's Pottery Road breeding machine. She was a small, soft female who kept producing kittens faster than we could find homes for them. Pamela, who had a statistical mind, once sat down with pencil and paper and figured out that Whisper had produced 120 kittens during her long stay at Maison Berton.

As a result of Whisper's fecundity, our home was swamped with kittens of various stamps. We had no sooner succeeded in giving away the last batch before another appeared, usually in my daughter Penny's sweater cupboard. Meanwhile other expectant mothers were making a beeline for our place. These included a striped female we named Candy (for candy stripe) who managed to drop half a dozen kittens at the same time Whisper presented us with her newest batch. Both mothers became confused. Neither knew which kittens were which, nor did the kittens themselves, who latched onto the handiest nipple.

The confusion increased as more cats began to arrive and take temporary or permanent quarters in our tool shed. Most of these were rough and ready males with torn ears and tails, but some were half-grown kittens who had no idea who their mothers were. They stole the food we set out for Whisper and Candy and fashioned makeshift nests among the coils of hose and boxes of discarded magazines.

We tried to keep them out but they managed to squeeze into our kitchen. Soon they were everywhere, peering out of closets, scampering over our bed at night, clamouring to get out, pleading to get in, clawing at the door, climbing the curtains, getting trapped in the furnace room, growling, howling, scratching, spitting, and purring when the mood struck them.

It was too much. They came and went as if they owned the place. We treated them as strays—didn't even give them names—but they acted as guests. A vagrant thought crossed my mind: What if something happened to us and we were found dead in our own home surrounded by waves of hungry cats? I didn't want to make the front page that way.

As a result, Janet undertook the difficult task of figuring out how many cats were hanging around our place. To her astonishment the number came to seventeen. That was too much, and it led to the Great Cat Hunt in which we rounded up all the half-starved cats by offering them free grub and corralled them into the back of the station wagon. Next stop: Toronto Humane Society.

It was clear, however, that the time had come for equally drastic action. Our own pets were producing kittens at an alarming rate, eating us into the poorhouse. Was there no way that we could exploit them? A fiendish scheme was percolating in my mind. *Publicity!* Why not advertise our kittens for sale? Turn mothers like Whisper into money-making machines. I was writing a column for the *Toronto Star* at the time. So why not use *Star* classified ads to sell the kittens for big dough?

 ## THE GREAT KITTEN SALES SCHEME

I entered into this scheme full of starry-eyed optimism. But like so many similar endeavours it didn't quite work out the way I expected. Here is the report I made to my readers. It was, of course, partly in jest, but there was also a hard core of truth at the centre of my account:

Like most newspapermen, I glow all over when the paper to which I extend my loyalties gets a clean beat (or "scoop" as we journalists call it) on our hated rivals.

A beat or scoop is a story that we publish which the other papers haven't got. We run several every day, some under flaring headlines, others concealed more modestly in the back pages.

It is these more modest yet undeniably exclusive stories that intrigue me. One, for instance, which seems to appear every day, never gets into the other papers. It is the one headed "STAR WANT ADS GET RESULTS," and I never tire of reading it.

It is different every day, of course. One day it will have a scoop about how H. Reinflesch of Apt. 2B, 415 Grool St., got no less than 215 calls when he decided to part with his collection of fine old tuning forks. Another day it will tell the heart-warming human interest story of Mrs. G. Flaub who, by inserting a simple two-line ad in the Articles for Sale column, was cleaned out of cyclo-massage pads in a matter of hours.

Well, I am sorry to have to report that I am at this moment on my way down to the Star Bureau of Accuracy with a couple of these clippings in my hand. If, as it says here, **Star Want Ads Get Results,** how come this Star want ad didn't get results?

> **For Sale:** Siamese kittens. Excellent
> blood lines; housebroken; affectionate.
> Fond of children

This ad was inserted on several occasions at my request, partly to test the true effectiveness of Star Want Ads and partly to get Siamese kittens out of my bed, out of my soup, off my lap, and out of my hair.

Affectionate! Ye gods, that is the understatement of the year. Three of them are sitting on my typewriter as I set these words to paper.

And yet this Want Ad, conservatively worded, with no suggestion of hard-sell, telling the simple truth, and appealing to the pet-loving and snobbish instincts of Star readers, has had no result at all. I might as well warn our Classified Department that the *Globe* and *Tely* have been phoning in some pretty attractive offers, not for the kittens, understand, but for ads in their papers at cut prices.

I am an unashamed cat lover. I have always owned cats and I always will own cats. Sorry, Bureau of Accuracy, I got that wrong: cats have always owned *me.*

The trouble with cats, however, is that they multiply. And it is not so easy to give away kittens, even as door prizes at parties, a trick I have resorted to on certain desperate occasions.

That is when I hit upon the idea of exchanging all our cats for pure-blooded Siamese.

"If we are going to raise cats," I said to my wife, "the thing to do is make something of it. Why force mongrel kittens on people when Siamese fetch top prices? Some people breed rabbits and end up wealthy. We will breed cats! Instead of pleading with people to take our cats, people will plead with *us.* They will bring money, even."

This explains why our house at the moment is full of Siamese cats. They are everywhere. The cupboards are full of them. Several are sleeping on my ties. Two are living in the oven. They hang from the trees like ripe fruit and they sit at the table with bibs on waiting for supper. A fleet of Dr. Ballard's trucks moves in a constant stream from the factory to our kitchen, bringing tins of horsemeat by the case lot and invoices twice monthly.

Somehow the great cat development scheme has flopped. The cats have done their part nobly. But the public has not responded.

Peter with Princess Paprika of Kowloon

I suspect that the Siamese Cat business is like the pyramid clubs. For a while the Siamese was the Status Cat; if you didn't have one, you were Non-U. Now the saturation point has been reached, but the cats don't know it. One of our nursing mothers, I notice, seems to have got herself pregnant again.

The Cat Club is going to call me a fink, I know, but if I don't get a response soon I am going to have to cut prices or cut throats. Meanwhile, if there's anybody around desperately in need of affectionate kittens with excellent blood lines, I know where such can be obtained. And if the Star Want Ad department wants to bill me for this space, let them do their worst.

THE CATS THAT BETRAYED ME

For several months I persevered in a mammoth Siamese cat program. But my scheme to make a modest living as a cat breeder fell apart because the cats themselves refused to co-operate. Once again I resorted to my column, this time as a kind of apology for the preceding one. And, as before, there was more than a grain of truth in it. Here is what I wrote:

> *It pains me more than I can convey, to have to report*
> *that my long-term experiment in Siamese cat breeding*
> *has ended in utter and absolute failure. Lord knows,*
> *I've tried but I reckoned without the independent*
> *mind and general stubbornness of the Princess Sari*

of Shan Ling, famous houseboat traveller and mother of eighteen.

The graduating class will recall that, early in our studies, I provided a detailed history of Cats I Have Known in order to explain why I was getting out of the Mongrel Cat Business and into the Expensive Purebred Siamese Cat Business.

I say "business" because there have always been too many felines around our place to designate by the simple name of "pets." When we get a cat at our place we get more than just a cat. We get the cat's uncles and aunts. We get the cat's casual acquaintances. We get the cat's boyfriends, all of them highly argumentative. Sooner or later we get the cat's offspring.

The trouble with all these cats was that they did not understand the population explosion. I didn't so much mind the cats who eloped; it was the cats who came home with new brides who bothered me. You can only give away so many kittens as door prizes at parties before your friends start thinning out.

And I have never been much good at drowning kittens. By the time I screw up enough courage to do it, the kittens have started to purr and that defeats me. Indeed, the only people who can drown kittens without a qualm are sweet elderly ladies. They seem to have a special knack for it which has eluded me.

The solution to the cat problem at our house came to me with blinding clarity one summer midnight: If *we must be overrun by cats, why not by expensive cats? It we* must *be in the cat-breeding business, why not breed cats that* sell? *In short, why not cash in on the big craze for Siamese, the Status Cats of the Sixties?*

The plan went into effect that summer, though not without difficulty, since it took some time to persuade all the Low Status cats to leave. We went through a pretty hectic time discouraging new cats while waiting for nature to take its course with the old ones. Eventually, the time came when we had no more cats. It was then that we acquired, at enormous expense, two Siamese kittens. The Great Cat-Breeding Program had begun.

Siamese cats, as you may know, are different from ordinary cats. For one thing they cost money. For another, they really do think they are dogs; we have always had problems trying to stop them from following the children to school. They are affectionate, graceful, and very noisy. They howl, not because they are hungry, thirsty, sex-mad, or unhappy, but simply because they insist on taking part in the general conversation. You get used to it after a while.

They have also been influenced heavily by that school of artists who devote themselves entirely to making decorative paintings of Siamese cats. Our cats were always striking attitude, arranging themselves in arabesques or playing the part of bookends. I like it when they do this; it beats the howling.

As the cats grew up we waited for a beautiful friendship to develop between them. They seemed to

get along well and the time came when the Princess
Sari had a litter of chalk-white kittens. People actually
fought to buy these at prices as high as $35 per kitten. I
figured I had it made since we had paid out very little
more than that in cat food, vitamins, cod liver oil,
rabies inoculations, and distemper shots. It was mere
child's play making out their pedigree papers; a couple
of full-time secretaries working around the clock got
that job done inside a week.

It was about this time that we noticed our male cat,
Simon of Athens, sneaking out at nights. I actually caught
him chasing a handsome tabby through the bushes one
morning. His absences from home grew longer and
longer, and then one day he just didn't return. We
heard vague reports of his co-habiting with a blonde
in a barn over on the next concession. Then silence.

At about this time I became vaguely aware of a general increase in the Non-Status Cat population around
our place. Handsome devil cats began popping out of the
bushes tipping their hats and leering at the Princess Sari.
Slavering yellow monsters would come sliding through
the bedroom window, after first carefully removing their
shoes and stockings. Soon the place was crawling with
male cats—and crawling is the proper word.

We got the Princess out of there fast. We
spirited her off to an enormous cattery where for
a mere $50 she was engaged with a giant Siamese
in whose veins the blood of a dozen champions

flowed. Two days later we reclaimed her and awaited developments.

The developments arrived, in due course, mewing lustily. One was jet black. A second was a beautiful brown. A third was a sort of yellow. A fourth was a soft gray. A couple of others seemed to have a touch of Persian in them, but we couldn't be sure.

That was some months ago. Since that time the Princess has presented us with two more litters in assorted colours. The house is alive with kittens: the spirea is crawling with toms, awaiting to pounce; and we are planning another party—with door prizes.

SIX

Whisper's Kin

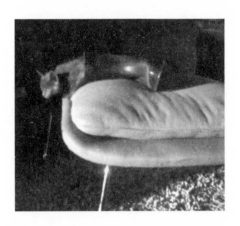

THANKS TO WHISPER, THE CHAMPION MOTHER, THE KITTENS kept arriving and so did gift cats, like the two Siamese we received at Christmas because the owner's daughter was allergic to cat fur. These were two handsome sealpoints whom my No. 3 daughter, Patsy, named Winston and Julian. That was a pleasant change from Frisky, Fluffy, and Cuddles. They were big, proud sealpoints and I honoured her for giving them names to go with their feline dignity. How did she arrive at such names? I asked her and she replied, without a pause, that "Winston" was named for Winston Churchill and "Julian" for Julian Caesar. Magisterial! Showed the child was benefitting from her history classes, even though she got Caesar's first

Julian at war with Whisper the kitten

name wrong. Only years later did I realize that they were named, not for the two great classical figures, but for John Winston Lennon and Paul Julian McCartney.

 ## NEFER'S MASQUERADE

The Great Cat Hunt did little to reduce our cat population. Thanks to Whisper, the kittens kept arriving at regular intervals. Cats and kittens, mongrels and purebreds became indistinguishable. The whole lot slept together in a great furry mound, usually on the kitchen ironing board.

We kept running out of names for the new arrivals, having long used up all the condiments and spices. Higher education helped out. Pamela's cat was called Nefer, a shortened version of Nefertiti, the ancient Egyptian queen. Penny had two from

a later batch of Whisper's whom she called Eros and Agapé, since she was taking a course on Greek love at college. The cats did not go to college with their owners but lived free at our place, perfectly at home with their many half-brothers and cousins.

Nefer was the most handsome cat of the lot, a soft grey-blue from head to tail with a soft grey temperament to match. When Winston and Julian occasionally got into an argument, Whisper, who was half their size, would intervene physically until she calmed them down. But Nefer did not deign to become involved.

One afternoon, a distant cousin arrived on a visit with a group of young friends. I was appearing regularly on *Front Page Challenge* in those days, and I suspect she had brought them to our house to show off and ask the usual questions: Is the show fixed? What is Gordon Sinclair *really* like? The centre of attraction, however, turned out to be Nefer, who wandered majestically into the living room and found a spot exactly in the middle of the circle of admirers. There he sat, bolt upright, like one of those Egyptian cats you sometimes see in illustrations—impassive, imperious, and peacock-proud.

"What a beautiful cat!" someone said. "It looks like she's kinda special."

"*Very* special," I said, glad to have the spotlight shift.

"What kinda cat is he?"

OPPOSITE: *Nefer standing tall beside a mound of felines on our ironing board*

"Why, he's a rare Abyssinian Blue," I extemporized. "A *Royal* Abyssinian," I added.

"I never did see one of those before."

"No. It's unlikely you have."

"Kinda rare, are they?"

"Just about the rarest cat you can have."

"Really? Wod'you mean?"

"There are only six of these in Canada," I told him. "You've got to be careful how you breed them. The Royal Abyssinian Cat Society is very particular about that."

By this time everybody had their eyes on Nefer, who had adopted his bored look for the occasion.

"Could I, like, maybe *touch* him?" one asked.

"Be careful," I said. "The Royal Abyssinians are very touchy."

Nefer raised his chin and allowed it to be tickled.

"That's just amazing," I said. "Royal Abyssinians don't take to just anyone; especially the Royal Blues. It's not often they allow you to pet them. He must have sensed something."

Someone else reached out to touch the cat, who played his role brilliantly, averting his head and opening his eyes wide. The visitor drew her hand back as if she'd touched a red-hot stove.

"Only six in Canada?" someone asked.

"That's right. Two in Victoria, one in Regina—a wealthy rancher paid to get her there. One here. One in Montreal. And one, I think, around Windsor. I'm not sure of that. But I must tell you that you've just seen something that very few people in this country have had the privilege of viewing."

As I spoke, Nefer stretched, turned, and slowly stalked out of the room heading for the kitchen.

After the visitors left, oohing and aahing, I gave the fake Abyssinian a saucer of pure cream as a thank-you offering. Nefer had made their day, and mine too.

In his youth, Nefer was a mighty hunter: voles, marmots, mice, chipmunks, even baby rabbits were his prey. Sometimes, however, his instincts went too far. He was, like most cats, an accomplished birdwatcher, but the birds he watched always eluded his grasp and mocked him shrilly from the tops of trees. There was one exception, however, and the results were lamentable.

One Christmas we decided to surprise Peggy Anne, aged six, with a special gift. We picked a beautiful canary from a downtown pet shop and brought it home in a cage. It wasn't easy to keep the present a secret, because the canary was in full throat when we arrived on Christmas Eve. But we concealed the cage in the broom closet and waited the long wait while we tried to get Peggy Anne to sleep—a difficult endeavour with the radio playing "Silent Night, Holy Night."

Finally, out of the closet came the caged canary and into the living room came Nefer—not sauntering, in his usual grand fashion, as befits a Rare Abyssinian Blue, but legging it for the cage, which Pamela managed to snatch from him. Obviously we couldn't put Peggy Anne's Christmas present under the tree. We would have to screw a large hook into the ceiling and suspend the cage and canary high above the waiting cat.

The task was completed at last, and the stockings hung on the chimney with care. Canary and cage were hoisted eight feet above the floor, safe from the marauder who paced restlessly below, eyes agleam. When we settled back to fill the last of the stockings, Nefer settled back to stare hungrily at the cage above him.

Suddenly, when my hands were full of candy canes, he gathered his loins and launched himself at the ceiling. Before I could stop him he had managed to cling to the bottom of the cage by his front paws, causing it to swing like a pendulum. With the canary shrieking blue heaven, Nefer performed his flying trapeze act, pumping with his hind legs until he managed to pull the bottom of the cage free. The cat landed with a thud on the carpet. The shrieking bird landed on the cat then streaked down the hall, a yellow blur. It was an uneven contest. Nefer had the canary in his clutches long before it reached Peggy Anne's room, at which point the Royal Abyssinian Blue enjoyed a hearty meal of canary. We didn't have the heart to break the ghastly news to Peggy Anne.

Nefer, the canary hunter, was almost indistinguishable from another of Whisper's offerings. This was Agapé, a beautiful blue cat from another litter who, with his sister Eros, officially belonged to Penny. The only way you could tell Agapé from his half-brother, Nefer, was that Agapé continually sucked his tail, a fetish none of us could break. It was rare to find him without his tail in his mouth. As a result it was always stringy, like a rat's—not very attractive, but useful for identification purposes. One day, at the end of summer, Penny went off to college with Nefer, believing that she was taking Agapé home. Pamela had to race after her and make the exchange. The cats didn't seem to care.

 ## WINSTON AND JULIAN

Winston was another mighty hunter, like Nefer—the only cat in our long history who actually caught a ring-necked pheasant and brought it into the kitchen in his mouth, like a retriever. After a brief struggle, I snatched it from his jaws and placed it on top of the fridge, too high, I thought, for him to snatch it back. *Wrong!* Like Nefer, he executed a giant leap, seized it, and rushed off down the hall with his prey.

A second tussle followed. Once again I grabbed the pheasant and hid it inside the fridge. We had the bird for dinner that night (*delicious!*) while Winston sulked in the background. "Go out and get another one," I told him. He turned his back on me and strode off. We didn't see him again until the following day.

We farmed Winston out briefly to one of Janet's friends as a stud for a pedigreed bluepoint. He performed admirably and as a stud fee we received a handsome pure-blooded Siamese kitten we named Meow Tse-tung. We were building a farm pond on our property that spring and the little kitten would go down every morning to watch the bulldozer at work. He and Dave, the bulldozer man, became fast friends, and once Dave let him ride on the bulldozer with him. Because we were, as usual, up to our eyeballs in cats, we decided to make Dave a present of Meow Tse-tung whom, I regret to say, was growing into a bit of a bully. No doubt his affair with the bulldozer had something to do with it.

That summer Dave went away for a long holiday and asked if we might look after his cat during his absence. After all, Meow Tse-tung would certainly feel at home. Unfortunately, he felt so much at home that both Winston and Julian became jealous, especially when the visitor began to act as if he owned the place. Of course, Winston didn't recognize Meow as his own progeny; male cats rarely do. To the two brothers, he was a very pushy cat and a rather nasty one. So Winston and Julian simply ran away.

We heard about them from time to time. Neighbours reported seeing them together, flitting through the bushes in the valley. One local resident insisted that the pair had joined up with a gang of wild cats in the woods. I wasn't aware that such a gang existed, but discovered that there were indeed groups of strays living off the land that season.

I thought of Pousse-Pousse next door, who had returned home after an aerial adventure and a seven-month absence. Would Winston and Julian find their way back? More important, would they *want* to come back? They were both handsome males; would hikers wandering up the valley seize them and sell them for profit? I doubted that. These were canny cats, hard to catch. Harder to hang onto. But they were also determined to go their own way without interference from the handsome but wicked Meow Tse-tung, who had taken over our household. Visitors would arrive and compliment us on his beauty and his lovely temperament. The charlatan would roll over, purr, let them tickle his belly, and generally act like a sweetheart. I knew better and so did Winston and Julian. He was putting on an act, lapping up the cat food, cozying up to strangers, playing the role of the Perfect Cat. He liked the free grub and warm bed in our establishment, especially when cleared of the presence of the rightful owners.

To my relief, Dave came back in the fall just as the trees were beginning to turn colour. I pleaded with him to take Meow Tse-tung off our hands, and he obliged. The cat, of course, had no say in the transaction. But how would Winston and Julian know? Was there some kind of cat telepathy that would alert them to the absence of the interloper?

Obviously there was, but it took some time before the news reached them. It was the approach of winter that spurred them on. One morning, when the first frost appeared on the meadow, a shivering Julian turned up at our door asking to be let in. A month went by. Finally, it started to snow and there, shaking the flakes off his fur and clawing at the kitchen door, was Winston, acting as if he'd run away. No more stud fees for him.

IGNATIUS AND CRESSIDA

Agapé, Eros, and Nefer were a long time gone when Penny left home and moved with her boyfriend into a Toronto flat. But the memory of the two apparently identical blue cats certainly played a part in a confusing contretemps.

Penny now owned two new felines. One, a big handsome yellow male, was named Ignatius, while the other, a soft, grey long-haired female, was known as Cressida. (There was, at one time, another cat, Troilus, to match Cressida but the details of his demise are now fuzzy.) Ignatius got his name from Penny's boyfriend. To him, the word "ignite" described a cat that was perennially on fire. Cressida, a smaller, more nervous animal, had the eyes of a courtesan, with long lashes that she habitually batted at strangers. Penny thought of her as a feline Blanche Dubois, from *A Streetcar Named Desire*.

There came a time, however, when a temporary home had to be found for Penny's two cats while the painters were decorating her lodgings. Penny immediately thought of her friend, Vicki Filion, whose father, Harry, was my best friend (remember the cat who looked like Hitler?). Years before, Harry had saved Vicki from the fleshpots of Vancouver by sending her to puritan Kleinburg, where she and Penny shared a room. That was sometime before she became Vicki Gabereau, star of national radio and TV.

Vicki was not a cat person, but a dog person. Cat people

like *any* cat—Manx, Burmese, tabbies, or plain mongrels—it doesn't matter. But Vicki and her family were nuts about dachshunds, and *only* dachshunds. I explain all that because Vicki knew very little about cats; and that was what caused the problem with Ignatius.

Penny duly arrived, as arranged, and dropped off her two cats in Vicki's living room. Vicki was abnormally busy at the time. Among other things, she was running for mayor of Toronto, garbed in a clown suit and calling herself Rosie. For another, she was appearing on a Brampton radio station whose call letters—CHIC—had persuaded the owner to hire only women. "CHIC—where the girls are" was the slogan. So Vicki

Cressida (left) and Ignatius sit for their official portrait

accepted the cats, then went off to Brampton to do girl talk on the air, leaving them alone at home.

But not for long. Vicki's upstairs tenant soon arrived, to discover two very strange and very addled cats trying to come to terms with their new lodgings. He was definitely not a cat person. To him they were strays. He picked up the supposed interlopers and threw them out the front door.

When Vicki returned and discovered that Penny's two pets were missing she was panic stricken. "Penny will *kill* me!" she kept saying over and over again to anyone who would listen, as she searched aimlessly up and down the street for the missing pair. What had happened to them? Where had they gone? And how would she explain this tragedy to Penny?

We know what happened to Cressida. When she finally turned up at Vicki's front door, exhausted and hungry, Vicki reconstructed her odyssey with the help of some neighbours. This was a typical Toronto suburban street where every house looked like every other house: same front porch, same front lawn, same twenties style. Cressida was baffled. Which of these identical domiciles was the right one?

She trekked from door to door, mewing to be let in, only to be rejected as a stray. She had been thrown out of one house; now she was being thrown out of others, or was it the *same* house? She couldn't tell. Time after time the door was opened for her and time after time she was turned away. She wandered, baffled, up and down the street, hoping wistfully to be welcomed in and each time found herself rejected. Finally, by an exhausting process of elimination, she found herself on Vicki's front porch, and her long adventure was at an end.

But what of Ignatius? As the days passed, Vicki began to realize he was gone for good. What to do? She couldn't bear to face Penny and report that her beautiful yellow pet had vanished. At last a brilliant scheme evolved in her mind. Why not replace the missing Ignatius with *another* yellow cat? Penny, she remembered, had once confused Agapé with Nefer. To Vicki, the dog person, all yellow cats looked the same. The thing to do was to advertise around the neighbourhood offering a reward for a big yellow male.

Pretty soon a series of small boys began to arrive at Vicki's door, lugging tawny felines of various shapes and sizes, and demanding the loot. Vicki had no idea there were so many cats like Penny's in her neighbourhood. Some were large, some were tiny, some were fat, some were scrawny. Some were old and beat up, and some were still kittens. One or two looked good enough to pass for Ignatius, or so Vicki believed.

She was in the act of selecting a surrogate—in spite of a torn ear—when the real Ignatius strolled in, sat down and began washing himself free of the dust of the street. It was, as Vicki said later, a close call. She did not get around to telling Penny the whole story for some time, nor did she again agree to provide board and lodging for any of her friend's cats. But she did learn the hard way that all yellow cats are not alike.

INTERLUDE

Cat Houses

 CLUB CAT

When my daughter-in-law explained that there was "a luxury hotel for pampered felines" on the outskirts of Vancouver, I had to see it. I imagined a series of cages with cats pacing about inside and howling for their dinner. I didn't expect a nightly turn-down service, television, a spa, suites with double beds, and gourmet food on demand. But that's what I found when Club Cat's big stretch limousine picked me up and drove me to a kind of cat heaven in Cloverdale.

"Used limousines are a drug on the market," Jim Bell, the driver and co-manager of the club, told me as we drove off. "This one was cheap. We often pick up cats at the airport; they love the ride." In the extra seat at the back, my companions— two enormous stuffed felines (the kind you win at fall fairs and carnivals)—stared at me through glass eyes.

Cats in cages? Forget it. Club Cat provides everything for cats that human beings insist on at a luxury spa. Jim's boss and companion, Brenda Smith, who thought up the idea, greeted me as we pulled in, and a moment later we were inside the white-latticed building, which that day was host to fourteen cats of various shapes and sizes. Each had his or her own luxury suite, complete with everything from mini-bar and souvenir soap to a bottle of Cat Champagne on the end table. I got the impression that some of these extras had been put in place to lure cat lovers rather than cats, but there's no doubt the cats themselves enjoyed the attention.

"Every time I come in here I have to laugh," Brenda remarked with a chuckle. She chuckles a good deal these days.

I peered through the door of the nearest suite and there, slumbering peacefully on twin beds with matching pink coverlets, were two tawny and obviously pampered cats. In the balcony above, easily reached from the suite, a blue Persian roamed, peering cautiously down at us. Other cats occupied adjoining suites, doing what all cats love to do—come in, go out, and come in again, endlessly.

"I've always loved cats," Brenda told me. She got her first Siamese, Princess Anastasia, when she was twelve. She remembered when the family moved to Toronto, leaving Ana in a cage at the vet's. "She didn't eat for ten days and was a wreck when we came home." In those days there was no Club Cat to ease her loneliness. So now Brenda runs one.

In Brenda's hotel, guests are treated like royalty from the moment they arrive. Indeed, there is a Royal Suite available. There is, in fact, something for everybody. In the Honeymoon Suite there's a waterbed covered with an electric heating pad that visiting cats enjoy. In the Sports Bar, there's a piano on which the guests can thump their paws and a tiny television set that shows tapes, twice daily, of movies about various birds, complete with songs. The cats go crazy over that.

The Circus Suite is on two levels—complete with a trailer built to transport lions, and once used by a real circus—as well as a fortune teller's booth.

The walls of the Jungle Suite are decorated with small trophies—not lion's and leopard's heads, but a stuffed half-mouse and a half-rat, and the front half of a toad.

The Oriental Suite is decked out like a rickshaw with a bed on an elevated platform (like a litter), supported by poles.

The spa has a grooming centre complete with brushes and hair dryers, as well as a treadmill (on which the cats prefer to sleep) and several mirrors for those who like to admire themselves after being groomed.

At night only the front door is locked. The guest suites are always open so that the guests can come and go freely, as cats are wont to do. And each suite has a back entrance leading to a large screened area where the cats can sit or gambol in the sunshine.

The cats may not care about the decor as long as they get their food and catnip, but their owners take it all very seriously. One woman left her cat, Charlotte, at Club Cat and went off to England. She worried so much about Charlotte's situation that she phoned her mother in White Rock, near Vancouver, and asked her to check on Charlotte. She was worried that Charlotte would be in the Safari Room and not the Nautical Room. As for the Royal Suite, she felt that was too boring for the cat. The adjustments were made, and Charlotte was happy.

Royal Suite, Club Cat.

A lilacpoint takes his ease in a double bunk at Club Cat

These Balinese kittens were born just after I visited Club Cat

Brenda Smith's story has some of the quality of a soap opera. Before she started the Club five years ago, she'd tried everything without success. She'd been a bank teller until the bank was held up. She'd operated a maid service in Calgary and later another in Vancouver. She'd been manager of a dry-cleaning firm. She'd even travelled east to take a course toward becoming an air-traffic controller. That didn't work out either. When she looked ahead at twenty-five years spent checking on aircraft, it looked terribly boring.

There was something else: for most of her life she had suffered from bouts of black depression. Now she found herself spending too much time in bars and smoking pot. She was broke; she was lonely; she had been divorced three times, and her life was a mess. The only solution seemed to be suicide. As she puts it, "I was so disturbed I decided to check out."

There was one hitch. How could she leave her cats? One had stayed with her through all three divorces. It occurred to her that the only thing that made her laugh during those dark periods was the sight of a group of kittens playing in the barn. She had grown up with cats—once had ten of her own. Now it occurred to her that some sort of cat business would not only allow her to find a vocation she liked, but also help her cope with her depressions.

She had met Jim Bell in a pub in Langley. It turned out that he liked to train animals. He was also handy with tools. When she acquired her first breed cat, a skittish female named Delilah, he built a home for the expectant mother, called Do-Little House. It was from this small platform that they finally launched Club Cat.

They did no market research. "We followed the old saying:

'If you build it they will come.'" It took eight months before the new building, which Jim Bell put together, began to fill up. Then the bookings poured in. By the time I visited Club Cat, Brenda was turning down at least five potential guests every day; at Christmas she has had to turn away as many as fifty. A second cat hotel was built in the summer of 2001; three more are in the planning stage.

It costs $17 a night to keep a cat at the hotel—another $13 for an additional guest. Extended stays run to $300 a month. One client, Ken LeFolii, a former editor of *Maclean's,* boarded his cat at the club for a year and a half, rather than subject it to the lengthy quarantine process that would be involved during his long sojourn in Australia. Nor is it unusual for cat owners to phone their pets long distance during a European vacation to make sure they're reasonably content, though I suspect the cats aren't too good on the phone.

Club Cat gave Brenda a purpose in life. "I've had depressive episodes since I started it," she admitted, "but for the last four years suicide has not been in the plan. I *couldn't* leave the cats; they needed me. I was only going to stick around if I was having fun. Now I'm having fun. I put hats on cats, put kittens on Christmas trees, bought a kiln, cat moulds, and a sewing machine."

She taught herself to sew and makes doll's clothes for those owners who want to dress up their cats. "I broke fifteen needles in the first hour," she remembered. She grows her own catnip and grinds it in a coffee grinder for her feline guests. With her new kiln, she makes ceramic toys for cats to play with, and sells her own soap which is wrapped as a souvenir, complete with cat pictures on the label. Everything in Club Cat, from the pictures on the walls, to the handmade covers on the bunk beds has a cat motif.

Brenda calls herself the black sheep of a strict missionary family. In dreaming up Club Cat, she admits, she was rebuilding her childhood. "Do-Little House was my 'fort.' Club Cat was my dollhouse. It was like Noah's Ark in the making. I was laughed at, pitied, and received tactful suggestions regarding medication." Her family wasn't much help. "Mental illness and drug use are the instruments of the devil, apparently, and if I would just get right with the Lord I would be well.

"But without the 'illness' would I have invested all the money, time, and energy I had to put into an unproven idea? Somehow, I doubt it."

She walked around the building with me to show me the screened pen at the rear. I looked through the wire and a black Persian looked back at me and playfully poked his paw through the netting, just like Happy in the old days. I poked a finger back at him and he responded. It made me feel good.

Behind me, Brenda Smith started to chuckle. I thought of what she'd told me as a couple of other cats approached the screen to stare at me curiously.

"You guys are lifesavers," I said, as one extended a paw, and again Brenda chuckled, as she has chuckled regularly ever since Club Cat was born.

THE CATS OF PARLIAMENT HILL

I am walking west, just past the Centre Block looking for the cats' own parliament buildings in the shadow of the Peace Tower. Cats living on Parliament Hill? Indeed. It is a tradition that goes back, so I'm told, before the days of John A. himself. I follow a narrow asphalt walk just below a small wooded slope and there, stretched out on the walk and sunning themselves in the noonday light, are the fabled felines. One jumps into the lap of a visitor seated on one of the viewing benches. Two more jump on me and demand to be petted.

On the left of the path is a wire fence and behind it I note a long, low dormitory, its roof vaguely shaped in the chateau style so familiar to Ottawa visitors. Through a series of small doors, I can see cats of various shapes and sizes coming and going, in and out, cat-fashion, and pausing occasionally to sample some of the strategically placed bowls of food and water. Other cats arrive to claw their way up trees, trying vainly to catch elusive squirrels or teetering along the peak of the dormitory roof, while others lie about, grooming themselves obsessively.

Where do these cats come from? How long have they been here? Who looks after them? I get the answers from an amiable retired French Canadian, René Chartrand, who for the past fifteen years has taken it upon himself to care for the cats of Parliament Hill. René is more than a cat lover. He is, in truth, the cats' slave. Every single day of those fifteen years—

holidays, weekends, vacation time—he has come up here for two visits to look after the cats; and he has never missed a visit. He's eighty years old now, an ex-RCAF flyer, long since retired. These cats are his life. In the summer he spends between five and eight hours with them each day; in winter, at least three or four. Sometimes visitors leave money to help him out; local veterinarians work for him without charge; the cats endure, as they always have.

I talk with René as the cats swirl around my ankles. Long before he took over this task, he tells me, he used to come up here to see the cats who were then being overseen by an elderly woman, Irene Desormeaux. It was she who extracted a promise from him that, should anything happen to her, he would replace

her as the cats' benefactor. When she grew too ill to care for them, he took over.

During René's tenure, the cat population has grown. At this moment, twenty-four occupy the dormitory, but René tells me that he sometimes has as many as thirty-two on his hands. Even as a small boy, he remembers, there have always been cats living here just west of the Centre Block. Some tour leaders claim that the present inmates are descendants of those brought from England by Lt. Col. By himself, to control the mouse and rat population during the building of the Rideau Canal.

One thing is certain. The cats on Parliament Hill never roam, never leave home. Why should they? They've got it made, right here, where the nation's heart thumps proudly. Most are born here. All are tame enough and friendly enough to allow visitors to pet them and pick them up so that in their turn, they can lick the visitors. They are a very self-satisfied group of cats—what cat wouldn't be? René himself, with the help of a couple of friends, built the dormitory, a miniature Parliament Buildings, containing twelve two-cat apartments, which, in the winter, are insulated with hay.

I talk to René's assistant, Rob Roy, who tells me that René is a positively obsessive cat owner. When the cat population threatens to become too large, some cats must be taken to the Humane Society, but René resists that.

"We struggle with him," Rob tells me. "He's such a cat lover. He wants to keep them all. We try to convince him—but

OPPOSITE: *René Chartrand, the doyen of the cattery on Parliament Hill*

it depends on the cat. Like that white mother over there, right behind you on the wall. He looked at that cat and he said: 'She's staying!' So we finally said, okay. Incidentally, that's her son right there—the ginger."

René believes that all these cats are related in some way. Females in the group grow up and have kittens. Once the kittens are weaned the mothers ignore them—don't even recognize their own children. I look up at the soft white cat on the wall who is certainly paying no attention to her offspring. Indeed, as he stalks away she stares at him with what can be described only as a gesture of disdain.

In the early days Rob tells me, people used to drop off stray cats on Parliament Hill, but that has become a legal offence. Some visitors would like to adopt a cat, but René gets quite irritated when he's told about it. They are *his* cats; nobody else's. "He's got quite a temper when it comes to these cats," Rob says. "You don't even *suggest* adopting one."

Rob Roy, who claims descent from the original legendary Scot, got cat mania some years ago, quite by accident. "I was up here one night, sitting down on the bench, and didn't even see the shelter because it was so dark, when suddenly a cat jumped on my lap from out of nowhere—a real friendly cat. So I went over and I looked at all those cats, and I just started coming up here nights, just, you know, to visit during my walk.

"Then I had surgery on my hands so I was out of work for about two weeks. So I came up to see René every day and he slowly got me doing things for him, and I began coming up at lunch time. I have my own web design company so that allows me free time. If I want to, I can take two hours off in the afternoon and come up here and work." So Rob Roy was hooked. When René's not around, Rob is on duty.

René has names for all his cats—Pompom, Blackie, Blanchette, Fluffy, Garrison. Visitors turn up every day just to look at them and fondle them. The cats are always there, rarely straying far from their plates of food. They welcome new arrivals. "They just love it," René tells me. "They drive some people nuts because when they come up here the cats are all over them."

The toilers in the Parliament Buildings know them well. Pierre Trudeau, who enjoyed his walks, used to wander by. Brian Mulroney always waved from his limousine window. Journalists arrive occasionally—some from as far away as Venezuela—and television crews turn up to record the political cat phenomenon, if not for posterity, at least for a few fleeting moments on the tube. In good weather some 300 visitors a day find their way to the quiet enclave that is the domain of the cats of Parliament Hill. They are a never-ending attraction, albeit a minor one. But to real cat lovers, the life that vibrates here is far more rewarding than the kind on display nearby behind those granite Gothic walls.

 CAT CROSSING

As we initiates well know, the term "cat owner" is an oxymoron, like "military intelligence" or "friendly loan company." As I have tried to suggest in these pages, we cat lovers do not own our cats; our cats own us. From the moment they are born, cats are in control of the household. We indulge them and obey their orders. It is no use ignoring their commands, as I well know. A cat will get in the house no matter what steps you take to keep him out: He will climb over chimneys, as Sebastienne did, or claw his way up the eaves, like Happy. If you stubbornly try to sleep through his commands to release him for active duty, he will jump on your face, lick your ears, or even scratch you gently on the nose, as Pieface used to do.

Cats are cunning animals, far more cunning than dogs, and far more slippery. They will lurk in the shadows when they hear the door knob turn and slither out or in before you can slam the door shut. They will choose their own food and stubbornly refuse any other, and it's always a different brand, depending on the cat. They will seize control of the centre of the bed, making it impossible to wriggle into the covers; and they will glower at you if you try to move them. They have their own personal refuges—a chair, a carton, your favourite cushion—and they will defend it stubbornly from any rival cat. As Brenda Smith discovered in Vancouver and René Chartrand in Ottawa, the cats are always in charge, and their so-called "owners" are mere slaves.

The greatest slave of all is Jack Wright, a somewhat harried, sixty-five-year-old house painter who, when I visited him in Kingston, had no fewer than 480 cats living under his roof. That's right: *480 cats!* Jack is the cats' good and faithful servant. He spends eight hours a day at his house-painting job and another eight hours every day of the week on his cats. He takes no holidays—the cats wouldn't stand for it—and he's been at it for more than fifteen years. Of course, I had to meet him and I had to meet his cats.

Jack met me at the train and drove me to the house on Elm Street he calls Cat Crossing. As we approached the front door a dozen cats clawed their way up the screen to greet us. "They're crazy about strangers," Jack said, "but that's only for about fifteen minutes. After that they ignore you. You're just another piece of furniture."

But you can't ignore them. When Jack opened the door I was faced with a living wall of cats. The whole room vibrated with felines, clambering over me and over each other—*mounds* of them, drawers full of them, shelves covered with them, the very floor alive with them—a moving sea of tabbies and Russian blues, shorthairs and Persians, Maine Coon cats with huge tails, Angoras, Siamese of every shape and size, large cats, tiny cats, and drawers full of kittens peering out at me with their bright inquisitive eyes. I was afraid to move lest I accidentally squash a cat.

Here were cats sprawled on the floor, cats lying on tables or under tables, cats squatting on shelves and windowsills, cats

OVERLEAF: *Donna and Jack Wright, smothered in cats*

PIERRE BERTON

on the stove (mercifully unheated), cats in the bathtub and sinks, cats clawing at the door frames (which Jack has to change annually), cats on top of other cats, and cats cuddled together in furry feline piles—480 cats, in all, including those who leave the house through a back entry to make periodical trips in search of fresh air and sunlight in a 16 x 20 foot gazebo at the back.

Jack knows the names of all of them, such as Holly (born at Christmas), Angel, Number Seven (a black cat with the number in white fur on its back), Killer, Sylvester, and Sweetie. This last, a timid cat, has been living in one of Jack's closets for two years, too shy to come out. As a result Sweetie gets special cat food, an indulgence that has attracted two other cats who have moved into the closet with Sweetie to enjoy the extra attention.

Like Sweetie, all of the cats make gastrointestinal demands. "You won't believe that Siamese," Jack tells me, indicating a watchful cat on the table. "If you get canned tuna, it's got to be the best—Cloverleaf. And she won't eat regular ham; it's gotta be Black Forest. For the cats who want pork, we cook a roast every coupla nights. There are some who like only specialties. That Siamese there won't eat sirloin tip roast. It's gotta be eye of the round."

All the cats live on the ground floor of the Wright home. They are kept away from the basement and also from the second floor, which Jack rents out to a non-cat tenant. He certainly needs the rent money. The statistics involved in feeding 480 cats are awesome: three huge freezers containing eighty cases of meat, fifty pounds of dry food, and six litres of milk. Eight litter boxes have to be changed five times a day! Fifty pounds of ice are needed daily to keep the air conditioner working; the gazebo at the back requires fresh sod every month; and all the furniture must be sprayed twice a week with a mixture of ammonia, cleaning fluid, and water. That helps explain why Cat Crossing is remarkably free— but not entirely free—of the usual mixture of odours.

The question that haunted me when I first heard about Jack Wright and his myriad of cats was *why?* How on earth did he end up with a house crawling with that many? I have heard of cat lovers before, and have spent some time with several. I thought René had a surfeit of cats—but *this?* My mind boggles, my head swims as the curious cats pull at my trousers and try to climb on my shoulders, and rub up against me.

The facts are that Jack Wright was inundated with cats because he could not bear to reject them. The cats took over, as cats will do. He didn't intend to start out with hundreds of them; he just couldn't say no. His is a familiar saga, understandable to most cat lovers, who might easily whisper to themselves: "There but for the grace of God ..." You start with one lovely pet and, before you know it, his friends and relatives have moved in. Talking to Jack Wright brought back memories of that incredible mound of seventeen cats snoring on our kitchen ironing board. What if Janet hadn't taken matters into her own hands and carted them off? Would we now be enslaved by hundreds of cats?

It all began for Jack Wright in 1970 when he met a young waitress, Donna Belwa. When she married him, Donna brought along her black longhair—Midnight—as part of the contract. Midnight began to have kittens and the couple didn't have the heart to euthanize them. The inevitable followed. They took in a few more cats that others had given them. The Animal Foundation began to ask for help rescuing cats stuck on lamposts and in trees. Their owners didn't claim them and, to save them from the inevitable, the Wrights took them in.

By 1987 the cat population in their home had risen to 145; but that was only the beginning. When the supermarket tabloid, *National Enquirer,* held a contest to find out who had the most cats under one roof, a colleague entered the Wrights. Of course, they won, and the floodgates opened. People started dropping off unwanted cats in earnest, especially after Jack appeared on the popular "Phil Donohue" television show. Soon Cat Crossing was known in Kingston as a place to leave unwanted cats, and the Wrights' cat population began to explode.

Within three months the feline population in the Wright home had zoomed. Jack Wright, who keeps a careful count, told me at one period he was catering to 692 cats. 692! I couldn't get my head around that stunning figure. It seemed to me that the place was already crowded at 480; they must have piled up on top of one another. The cost of feeding them, he told me, drove him and his wife close to bankruptcy. He managed to reduce the number to 359 but, as I found when I visited him, the number was already creeping back up.

Unwanted cats turn up at Cats Crossing in droves. Few owners bother to knock at the door. One morning Jack found two kittens tied to a picnic table with a length of string.

Another time they discovered a box on their verandah and figured somebody had dropped off a gift of food. *Wrong!* In the box was a large pillow case and tied up inside was a mother cat and five kittens.

One woman called from Chicago after seeing the couple on TV. She'd just had a baby and her cat was so jealous it had started to wet her bed. "You've got to take it," she told Donna. "If you take it I'll send it up and send you a generous donation." After the cat was flown to Toronto the Wrights paid out $282 in wages, taxis, and airport fees. Inside the cat's box was a cheque for $25.

Other visitors are more generous. One woman of seventy dropped off seventeen cats at the Wrights' home, but continued to send a regular cheque for $200 more for their care.

For Donna, the cats became her life. She worked between twelve and eighteen hours a day, seven days a week, scrubbing and mopping, doing kitty laundry, wiping noses and giving medication while Jack hustled for work to pay for the ménage. Neither had any vacation, any new clothes, any new furniture, or draperies. Finally Donna moved out, leaving Jack alone with his cats.

But not quite alone. Donna still comes back daily to help out. Nor does Jack sleep alone; between 40 and 50 cats pile onto his bed with him, creating such congestion that, if he is forced to rise during the night, there's no space for him when he returns.

I met Donna Wright with Jack for lunch at a neighbouring restaurant. It was hard to believe that she had ever spent any time cleaning up after hundreds of cats. She is an extraordinarily neat little woman, impeccably turned out, her silver hair coiffed to the ultimate, her nails freshly manicured and painted, high heels, crisp lavender-blue top, printed skirt, and not a hair, a smudge, or a wrinkle to suggest a life spent catering to felines.

"Our day starts at six in the morning, cleaning and stuff," Jack had told me. "And then Donna does all the medication and the laundry. Matter of fact, I think she does too much. She's always got ten loads of laundry and every day she changes all the bedding. Me, I say 'Just flip it over.'"

He took me into a back room crowded with cats, of course. At one end, a bunch of kittens peeked out of a cardboard box. As they blinked at me, a calico cat happened by, took a look and proceeded to lick them all down. The mother? No, Jack told me, any passing cat will mother them.

"A bigger cat who likes a kitten will bathe it, no matter whose kitten it is," he explained, "and the bad thing is they steal them. You don't know where they are taking those kittens. A female will go by, see the kittens, and she'll grab them by the back of neck and away she goes—under the bed or somewhere. You know she's got a kitten and you'll hear the kitten crying, but you can't always find it."

Jack Wright's hobby, if you can call it such, has cost him money as well as time. The financial burden is awesome. At its peak, the bill ran to $100,000 a year, a sum made up from his painting job and donations. Jack has been forced to cut back but 480 is still a lot of cats. In the 2001 recession, the job opportunities began to decline and the donations decreased. Jack has had to take out mortgages and bank loans to keep Cat Crossing operational.

He's internationally famous. More than fifty reporting

teams have turned up at his door from places as varied as Beijing and Venezuela. But he's broke and mortgaged to his neck.

One way to help make ends meet, I think, might be to use this unique opportunity for academics to study the ever-mysterious felines. A remarkable thing about Cat Crossing is that the hundreds of cats, all confined to a single space, never seem to fight. This is astonishing and not only belies Brenda Smith's experience—that it's impossible to have more than twenty-five cats in one house without major trouble—but also flies in the face of animal psychologists the world over.

All these cats get along, and that's a miracle. "We've had letters from all over the world," Jack told me, "from England, from Europe, and the United States. All from psychologists who tell us that it's impossible for any more than twenty-five animals of any species to get along together. Really, I think it just depends how you treat them."

That's a simple answer but I suspect a careful investigation would reveal much more than that. Cat Crossing could make a valuable laboratory in which the most mysterious of all house-hold pets could be subject to careful analysis. And why not? It would provide extra funding for Jack Wright, while it's more than possible that science might unravel some of the more baffling aspects of feline existence (not to mention human).

And the cats themselves? As long as they get pampered with three meals a day of their own choosing, and a place to sprawl out, unimpeded, the cats wouldn't care.

SEVEN

Latter-day Cats

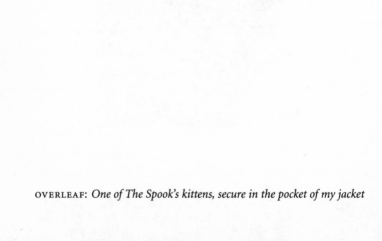

OVERLEAF: *One of The Spook's kittens, secure in the pocket of my jacket*

 TAIL LIGHT

The members of the great unwashed—by that I mean the non-cat people—are under the impression that all cats are alike. Nothing could be further from the truth. As we cat owners know, every cat is an individual, differing in every way from every other cat. Each one is unique. Their tastes, their attitudes, their habits, even their hopes and dreams bear little relation to those of their fellows. I know there are a good many theories about cats advanced by cat psychologists and veterinarians, but just as you think you've figured them out, your own cat does something to destroy them.

At this writing my wife and I are owned by three cats, all females, and all spayed now that my mother has gone to her rest. Each is a character, as different, one from the other, as a mouse differs from a gopher.

All three are shamelessly territorial. Tail Light, our Indoor cat, has appropriated the living room, dining room, and family room at the south end of our house. She rarely ventures down the three stairs that lead to the sleeping quarters. That is the domain of our In-and-Outdoor Cat, The Spook, who has appropriated my office, our adjoining bedroom, and, from time to time, our bathroom. The third member of this oddly assorted trio, Ruby, rarely comes into the house at all, but prefers to lurk outside, winter and summer, rain or shine, popping in only for the occasional snack. As I contemplate this curious trio, I look out the window and see Tail Light, our Indoor cat, who has actually ventured outside—a rare occasion—and is squatting on a bench below our big picture window, dreaming impossible dreams.

She arrived as a kitten, the gift of a friend, who wanted to assuage our grief over Clyde, who ventured too far afield and was struck by a car. We held a contest in the family to name her and the winning name was Mollie. But no one, except two of the grandchildren, call her that. She is a semi-long-haired tortoise-shell, brown and black, save for the tip of her tail, which is white. So we call her Tail Light because she is so easy to spot in the dark.

She has one endearing trait: she loves to answer the doorbell. As soon as she hears it ring, she pads off to greet the visitor and silently leads him into the house. If he takes a seat she perches beside him. She resists being petted. She doesn't even purr. But there she is, an amiable presence who plays no favourites: delivery boy, bill collector, old friends—all get the same treatment. When they leave, she accompanies them to the door, but stays behind when they say good-bye.

I am watching her as she sits on the bench overlooking the valley (the same valley where Pousse-Pousse was abducted). She came to us a tiny ball of fluff, but now she is a very large ball of fluff—a fat, bottom-heavy, lazy animal. She reminds me of one of those old-fashioned toys that used to delight us as children; we'd try to push them over but they always popped back up again because of the way the weight was distributed. That's Tail Light.

Now she is gazing up at the stone wall that leads to the roof and I can see her nether regions trembling as she gathers herself for a mighty leap. She is trying to imitate the feat of The

Tail Light in pensive mood—her only mood

Ruby bounding in the snow

Spook, our black cat whom she worships, but she hasn't got a hope. Some time ago she sat here watching with admiration as The Spook, in a single lithe move, leaped from the bench to the top of the wall and clawed her way upward to the nest of young starlings squawking on the roof. More birdie tartare for The Spook who made her way delicately down the wall, her appetite satisfied, as Tail Light watched helplessly.

Every day, on each of her ventures outside, Tail Light tries to emulate her mentor. Every day she gathers herself for the big leap and every day she abandons the effort and returns to the comfort of her favourite wing chair. She is the kind of cat who suffers chronically from the "slows," an affliction she sets aside only when her ears detect the sound of the can opener in the kitchen. Then, in an instant, the dreamer awakes, the sluggard transforms herself into an Olympic champion and streaks for the kitchen, skidding across the linoleum and besting her rivals by a good half-length, as she shoulders her way into the nearest dish.

 ## RUBY

If Tail Light is our Indoor Cat, Ruby is our Outdoor Queen. A handsome tabby, she is the sister of the lamented Clyde (I could not bring myself to call her Bonnie).

She is not one to snooze on a bed or sofa or even to howl for a tin of cat food. She likes the fresh air and, it must be acknowledged, she loves the small edible creatures who scuttle through the woods, winter and summer. Inclement weather holds no terrors for her. In the winter I have seen her bouncing from snowdrift to snowdrift in pursuit of Peggy Anne, whose studio is in an old caboose at one end of the property.

Ruby likes the outdoor life. Sometimes she lives in the caboose and sometimes under it, between the wheels. Once she got locked in for two days by mistake. She never complained but walked out majestically when Peggy Anne unlocked the door.

Where does she live? Where does she sleep? What are her haunts? In the thick woods that I planted behind the swimming pool? In the cedar forest, below our house? In the tall grasses of the adjoining meadow? I haven't the slightest idea. I only know that she never leaves our six-acre property, and that when I take my morning walk she is suddenly *there* like a grey ghost, trotting warily a few paces ahead of me, reading the ground like an infantry scout on the lookout for hidden enemies. Then, as I reach the door, she is suddenly gone.

Like most tabbies I have known, she is a survivor. The beautiful Himalayans last little more than a season in the country. They sit around the house looking gorgeous and admiring themselves. But outside they are goners. They fall into things. They cannot climb a tree. Nor do they watch over their shoulders as Ruby does. When she walks with me she is ever on the alert. She slips from sheltering bush to confining hedge. She never moves in a straight line across an open meadow, but navigates around the perimeter, concealed beneath a screen of foliage. Watch her now as she slips through the shrubbery border beyond the caboose. She stops, turns, looks back, looks forward, looks sideways, then moves swiftly across the next open space. A young husky dog from a neighbouring home once appeared and sniffed at Ruby. I never saw a cat move so fast—faster than even Tail Light at the sound of a can opener. Across the lawn she streaked, squeezed under the Lundy fence, and hurled herself into the comforting woods. She can scale a tree at the same speed. Like Wally Simpson, she is indestructible, which is more than you can say of our beautiful Himalayan, Og, who sat in the sun on the hill one late fall afternoon and was found the following spring, torn to bits by evil predators.

Ruby is totally independent, never asks a favour. She gets her own food—the dry kind she prefers—from a large pail in the corner of the kitchen. She never howls to get in as The Spook does, but waits patiently outside the door, slithers in when it's opened, and strides over to the food. Nobody has to feed her; she feeds herself, dives headfirst into the grub, eats her fill, and departs.

Tail Light sits there in the kitchen watching enviously. She, too, would like to jump into the pail. She clearly envies Ruby's agility and once, unable to resist temptation, she tried to follow her example. The result was disastrous. Ruby is as sure-footed as a squirrel. She teeters gracefully on the lip of the pail as she leans over to reach the grub. Tail Light cannot teeter; when she leaned over, she fell nose first into the pail, then tried vainly to claw her way out until we rescued her. Actually, she prefers tinned meat. She tends to worship Ruby and occasionally tries to make contact by leaping at her from the arm of the wing chair. On these occasions, Ruby ignores her and stalks off. She is the quintessential tabby—calm, resourceful, dignified, secure within herself.

Ruby, headfirst in the pail of dry cat food

 THE SPOOK

She is our in-and-out cat and she makes the most of it. She arrived on our doorstep one day without warning and proceeded to take over the house—a skinny little jet-black female whom Janet refers to as "the teenage cat." Unlike Ruby, who disdains sloppy sentiments, she is absurdly affectionate. When she arrived one morning, she acted as if she'd always lived here and made no bones about her desire to be petted, cosseted, and fed heartily.

We had no idea where she came from and no idea where, of a night, she went. She would vanish for two days and then turn up suddenly as if she'd never been away. She was a lissome female who looked like the black cats in the children's fairy stories—the kind who have just stepped off a witch's broom—for she was jet black from her ears to a tail that had the same kind of crook in it that you see on Halloween cats.

She didn't appear to have a bone in her body. Unlike Ruby, she didn't stride confidently, head held high; she *flowed*. She carried no identification and since she had adopted us we sent her to the vet to get the usual expensive shots. I called her Midnight and that was the name the vet always used. But there would be more bills after we learned where she came from and also where she went on those nights when she didn't lie sprawled on our bed, mewing for attention. Not far from the north edge of our property, across a gravel road there is a shaded driveway, winding several hundred yards through a conifer forest toward a distant house and a barn. Since the death of the owner, the property has been rented out to tenants and it was the small son of one of these tenants who told my daughter Pamela that the barn was full of cats. But, he hastened to add, Midnight, whom he called Tara, was not one of these. She belonged to the farmhouse, not the barn. Nobody seemed to care that she had adopted us.

Sometime later, we discovered that Tara was lactating. She had been pregnant, in spite of her slim form, and obviously had delivered. But where? When? Once again, the small boy was pumped for information. Yes, he said, this skinny teenaged cat had borne six kittens at the farm, but in the manner of all mother cats, she had moved them to an unknown location, and no one had been able to find them. He added that the cat's *real* name was The Spook. That certainly fitted and that is what we started to call her when, from time to time, she turned up.

Weeks went by. The Spook continued to arrive, demanding a free lunch, and continued to vanish—we knew not where. Were her kittens hidden somewhere along the laneway that led to the farm buildings? Were they hidden in the rafters? Anything was possible. Mother cats, as I well know, are the wiliest of pets, masters of the game of hide and seek.

It was our Scotch collie who unravelled the mystery at last, or perhaps was allowed, by The Spook, to unravel it. We were sitting out in the garden one sunny afternoon when he began to *point*—an odd gesture for a collie. We followed his nose and there, in the lee of our big limestone barbecue, on a small wooded slope, hidden in the tall grass, was a nest of

black-and-white kittens more than a month old and all gam-
bolling in the sun as their mother tried vainly to nudge them
back into the home she had made for them. There were six—
all as wild as tigers.

When I realized the logistics of the move that had brought
them here, my mind boggled. She had picked up each of her
kittens by the scruff of the neck, one at a time, and headed for
our place. Down the long driveway she went with the wriggling
kitten, then across the main road and into the woods behind our
swimming pool. There she would have had to squirm, kitten and
all, under the chain-link fence and make her way across the lawn
to the sequestered corner. That trek she would repeat at least five
times—more likely six, because mother cats cannot count.

The fierce dedication of mother cats never fails to impress
me. In my files there's a remarkable photograph from 1960 of a
tabby named Puddy, who bore her four offspring on a porch roof,
of all places, and then launched a series of airborne evacuations
to get them to safety. She would tenderly pick up one of the two-
day-old kittens in her teeth, teeter on the roof's edge and then
launch herself at the closest limb of a nearby tree. The *LIFE*
photograph shows her flying with a kitten locked in her forepaws.
Four times Puddy made the treacherous transfer and each time
she made a safe landing. There are many stories like that and The
Spook's own marathon belongs in such an anthology.

Our major task now was to try to tame The Spook's six wild
kittens. We used the only surefire method: we turned them over
to my two-year-old granddaughter. She cheerfully dragged them
about by any handy appendage—paws, tail, ears—and dressed

them in doll's clothes, so that, by day's end, they were all as docile as sheep. Little two-year-old girls are to kittens what Clyde Beatty was to the lions he lured into his famous circus cage.

The Spook was nothing if not prolific. Before we could get her spayed, she had four more kittens. And even as the vet was making sure she would have no more, he discovered another four embryos in her lithe and nurturing body.

She is, of course, in charge of the house. She has chosen our bed, which she insists is *her* bed. She doesn't sleep on a

The Spook on our bed, which she insists is hers

pillow or on one corner of the counterpane; she sprawls out in the very centre, making access and egress more than difficult. You cannot move her; she takes that ill. One has to wait until she demands to go out. Then we settle down, my wife and I, with the whole bed to ourselves at last, but only for a few brief hours. We have no sooner nodded off than we hear her outside, loudly demanding to be let in. What can we do? After all, she found us, and she's the boss.

 SUKI

There is a coda to this cat symphony. I was just putting the finishing touches to it when I heard a weird cry outside the bathroom window. It was a daunting sound—low, almost guttural—and it was *loud*. I thought back to little Wally Simpson, mewing shrilly from his perch in the weeping willow, but this was a different kind of cry, panic mixed with loneliness, a cry for help, if I ever heard one.

I stepped out the front door and looked about. The strange howling increased in volume. I looked down below the front stoop and there, caught in the bushes, was a tiny tabby kitten looking up at me and sobbing his heart out. Once again someone had dropped a cat on us—trekked all the way down our long driveway, deposited him at our front door, and fled.

I reached down and picked him up. His cries ceased as he

nuzzled into my arms and he began to purr. I took him into the house and tried to feed him, but all he wanted to do was to jump on me and rub against my face. He stared into my eyes, never blinking, and a vagrant thought crossed my mind. Could it be that this was the ghost of my first cat, Happy, come back to haunt me? I put that fancy aside; this cat was a softer grey than Happy, his markings less pronounced. His sharp features and big ears suggested Siamese blood.

Over the next few days one thing was certain: Of all the cats I have known and loved—the number goes well into the hundreds—this was the most affectionate little feline I had ever encountered. To meet him was to love him. He never stopped purring and he stuck to me, clinging like a drowning man to a life raft.

He never left my side, never stopped purring, climbed into our bed at night and slept between us, taking most of the pillow. He did not make strange with others. Anyone could pick him up without a struggle. He would lie back in the arms of any stranger and allow himself to be stroked and tickled. He was capable of crying, as I had learned, but he never uttered so much as a squeak. Whenever I sat down, he jumped on me, settled down, and dropped off to sleep. He slept anywhere, any time, in someone's arms, while lapping up his milk or while engaged in play. Suddenly—bam!—he would roll over and drop instantly to sleep.

He was too young and inexperienced to be cautious. When he wanted company, which was all the time, he got it. One morning when my wife was soaking in the big bathtub, he suddenly jumped in with a splash, nuzzled up to her soaking wet, and then tried to claw his way up the sides. She wrapped him in a big towel, but for the next while he looked properly bedraggled.

Suki as a kitten

We soon realized we could not keep him. Ruby, Tail Light, and The Spook were offended by the presence of a stranger in their house. When the kitten scampered up to Tail Light and tried to kiss her nose, the fat cat leaped a foot in the air, spit savagely at him, and fled. The Spook simply vanished for two days. Ruby refused to enter the house even for food, sulked in the caboose, and insisted on taking her meals elsewhere.

We knew he would have to go. Fortunately I had a fallback position—my literary agent, Elsa Franklin, whose own cat had suddenly died. I took the kitten to her and they bonded immediately. She calls him Suki and he rarely leaves her side.

I phoned her a day or two later to ask how the new arrival was doing. "I just love him," she told me. "He never stops purring. Everybody on the street loves him. There's one strange thing, though."

"What is it?" I asked.

"Well, he has this thing about water."

"Most cats have; they hate to get wet."

"No, no, it's nothing like that. He's *crazy* about water. He jumps into the bidet in the bathroom. He jumps into the kitchen sink. He tries to get into the shower with me. And he lies under any leaky tap that's handy and tries to lap up the drops as they fall. He's a unique cat."

"All cats are," I told her.

"Well, I've never known a kitty like this one. He's certainly the friendliest animal I've ever encountered. He seems too good to be true. I only have one question."

"What is it?"

"How the hell do I keep him from sitting on my head?"

CODA

FROM PAUL BERTON'S
Rules for Guests

From Paul Berton's **RULES FOR GUESTS**

III: CONVERSATION

After the usual greetings and pleasantries, please keep in mind the following rules for conversation in this household if you want anyone to listen to you.

1. *Ask regularly and repeatedly about the state of the household cats: what they eat, the state of their health, what funny thing they did today . . .*

2. *Punctuate your discussion of geopolitics, movies, or sex with stories about cats you have known (i.e., Yes, there is no question the situation in Belarus is volatile; that reminds me of the time a cat . . .)*

3. *No discussion is so intense, no story so riveting, no baseball game on TV so important, no kitchen task so crucial that it can't be interrupted when a cat enters the room. When one*

does, all attention should turn to the cat (i.e., Oh, what a beautiful cat, what's its name? That reminds me of the time a cat . . .)

4. If you do not own a cat, and in fact have hated and feared cats your entire life, do not disclose this information. Fake it, lie about your true feelings, and make up amusing stories about the felines you have known and loved.

PERMISSIONS

Every effort has been made to contact copyright holders. In the event of omission or error, please contact the publisher.

PAGES XIX, XXI: Anne Gordon

PAGES 1, 8, 10, 15: Reprinted with special permission of King Features Syndicate

PAGE 12: Reprinted with special permission of United Media

PAGE 13: © Tribune Media Services, Inc. All rights reserved. Reprinted with permission.

PAGE 93: Penny Berton

PAGES 102, 103: Brenda Smith

PAGE 114-115: Jack Chang, Kingston Whig-Standard

BOOKS BY PIERRE BERTON

ILLUSTRATED BOOKS
The New City (with Henri Rossier)
Remember Yesterday
The Great Railway
The Klondike Quest
Pierre Berton's Picture Book of Niagara Falls
Winter
The Great Lakes
Seacoasts
Pierre Berton's Canada

ANTHOLOGIES
Great Canadians
Pierre and Janet Berton's Canadian Food Guide
Historic Headlines
Farewell to the Twentieth Century
Worth Repeating
Welcome to the Twenty-first Century

FICTION
Masquerade (pseudonym Lisa Kroniuk)

BOOKS FOR YOUNG READERS
The Golden Trail
The Secret World of Og
Adventures in Canadian History (22 volumes)

ABOUT THE AUTHOR

Pierre Berton, Canada's most popular historian, has received three Governor General's awards for nonfiction, two Nellies for broadcasting, two National Newspaper awards, the Stephen Leacock Medal for Humour, and the National History Society's first award for "distinguished achievement in popularizing Canadian history." He holds fourteen honorary degrees, is a member of the Newsman's Hall of Fame, and is a Companion of the Order of Canada.